"You're A Genius — And I C̲a̲n̲ brilliantly combines the mind and spirit of an individual's unique learning system. Every teenager, teacher and parent should read this book. It teaches us a̲l̲l̲ how to do this.

June Thompson
Executive Director, California Association of Student Councils

"You're A Genius — And I Can Prove It! is perhaps one of the most important books available for our youth. It is a book that helps young people explore their choices, as well as 'empower' them with a strong sense of self. After all, what is more important than a young person's mind and sense of self? If children are to be our future, we must prepare them."

Gabriel Carteris
"90210" star

You're a Genius —
And I Can Prove It!

Unlock Your Natural Ability
To Achieve Excellence

Kimberly Kassner

Cartoons by Brian Narelle

EmpowerMind
Mill Valley, California

EmpowerMind
38 Miller Ave., Suite 201
Mill Valley, CA 94941
FAX: 415-389-6941

Cataloging-in-Publication Data

Kassner, Kimberly.
  You're a genius — and I can prove it! : unlock your natural ability to achieve excellence / Kimberly Kassner ; cartoons by Brian Narelle
  p. cm.
  ISBN 0-9642818-3-X
  Library of Congress 94-12045

  1. Learning, Psychology of.   2. Success—Psychological aspects.
  3. Motivation (Psychology)   4. Self-realization.   I. Title.

BF318.K37 1994   153.1'53

Cartoons by Brian Narelle
265-B Cascade Drive
Fairfax, CA 94930
415/457-3327
(Thank you, Brian!)

Printed in the United States of America
10 9 8 7 6 5 4 3 2

**To the young geniuses
who are not yet aware of the power of their minds
and the unlimited potential of their spirits.**

Genius

**"A guardian spirit allotted to a person from birth...
A *natural* talent or inclination."**

The inherent gifts you possess are the genius within you.

Acknowledgments

In 1990, my friend Diana DuBrow told me she had a vision of me writing several books and manuals. When she said that I would be doing "automatic writing" (an inspiration from God is how I understood it), I could only reply by saying, "Diana, I don't write; speaking is my thing." I spent the next few years learning, again, how to let go of limitations and follow my heart. Miracles continued to happen. And yes, I wrote and wrote.

Lourdes Billingsley helped me learn to trust and believe in myself more than ever before. She reiterated (until I finally got it) that it was up to me and me alone to make this book happen. In fact, within a week, five people unrelated to one another had visions of me writing this book and helping transform the way students in this country learn. You'd think I would've been elated. In fact, I was terrified! What a responsibility for one who "doesn't write." At that time, I hadn't yet developed the **EmpowerMind** course.

Then there are my remarkable editors: Karen Krigbaum, who had the toughest job: she did "edit number one." You know, making complete sentences. My next editor, a former school psychologist and retired director of special education provided me with my greatest test; thanks, dad. Once he got over the shock of realizing I could write (I know his feeling), he praised my work. Then, there was John Fremont, who edited the manuscript the final time. (That was the edit with the most rewrites.) John brought creative ideas to the format. He was an invaluable ally. Mark Gatter designed the cover and Cynthia Frank formatted the book and led me through the whole publishing process. Without them I would have been lost. Thank you! Thank you! Thank you!

Brian Narelle brought life to my words with his ingenious cartoons. He was there through the tough times with me, and was always supportive and creative. Then he topped it off with a great cover cartoon and logo.

Peter Earley went through the last stages with me. When I was frazzled and frustrated he hung in there, supporting and calming me. When I was losing my mind, he never gave up on me. He helped me edit and proof the book. He gave me opinions and insights, but most of all he loved me through the struggles and successes.

My parents, Fred and Eleanor, came in at the end to save the day! They funded the entire book project. Their belief in me means more than they will ever know. I could not feel more loved and supported. *Thank you!*

It was my best friend Sheila Bergner who helped me come up with the **EmpowerMind** name four years ago. Her support has been unending.

A special thanks to Nando Llacuna, the principal at San Rafael High School, because without his giving me a chance to prove myself, and his constant belief in me and **EmpowerMind**, this book might not have been written. He allowed me the opportunity for my first pilot study, and has supported me ever since. Because of him, I built credibility, and **EmpowerMind** flourished.

If Eddie Oliver hadn't pointed me in the right direction, I might not have had the opportunity to start working with our youth. I'll never forget him for that and for all of his support and encouragement to take off on my own.

My greatest thanks go to all of my wonderful students, teachers and parents, whom I have used as examples in this book, whose learning I have facilitated over the years. (Many of their names have been altered in this book to protect their privacy.) It was their courage to challenge themselves and me with their feedback that made **Empowerind** what it is today. Much love and thanks to Lily Merdita, Angel and Eric Rhoades for their commitment to learning **EmpowerMind**. They have time and time again been testimonials of the magic and transformations that can take place when one learns how to live the **EmpowerMind** course.

My other friends, Betsy Lovejoy, Brett Robertson, Scott Taylor, John Kassner, John Boas and George McClaird. Without your financial and computer support, I definitely would have crashed. Thank you for your faith in my vision.

Most of all—thank you from my heart, all of you, and all of my other friends, for your constant love.

— Kimberly

Table of Contents

Teach a child—create a student.
Empower a child—change a society.
Empower our youth—transform the world.

— *Kimberly Kassner*

Introduction

Unleash the unlimited power of your imagination and let the magic begin.

EMPOWERMIND. EmpowerMind is not just a book, a workshop, an audio tape or a video—it's a lifestyle. By simply reading this book, you will gain the essence of **EmpowerMind**; but if you truly want to grasp the potential of your mind, you *must implement* what you've learned. When you practice **Empower-Mind**, miracles happen—this is a guarantee! If you want your life to be a successful adventure, **EmpowerMind** *is* your answer but *only* with *your commitment*. Your life is about choices. Your road to success may have had detours in the past. Or were those detours simply adventures in disguise? *The choice has always been up to you!*

Join me on this journey, the **EmpowerMind** journey, where your imagination is reinforced and encouraged. You will gain a greater understanding of who you are, what you want and how to get it. **EmpowerMind** is a new way of approaching life. Any questions?

"Hey, isn't it also like what the pioneers did when they came West? And don't forget exploring new worlds and ahh...seeking out new life and new civilizations and boldly going where no man has gone before. And what about Beevis and Butthead...?"

That's my student, Hacker (that's his nickname, of course). Hacker is a genius, just like you are. He's one of my star high school students who took the **EmpowerMind** course. He's got real short hair with a small tail (on the back of his head, that is). He wears baggy (I mean *huge*) pants, old T-shirts and tennis shoes. As his friends say, "He's *radical!*"

"I told Kimberly I could help her talk to my peers (That's you, guys...and babes), so they would pay attention to her. So, let me just say I'll be along for the ride, commenting here and there and trying to keep Kimberly in tune to what's happenin' in our world. EmpowerMind works, man! I even chose to repeat the course three times because it was so much fun. I didn't believe it could work—or at least not for me. I'd given up on myself, and on all of my teachers."

Every so often Hacker reminds me to get back on track with teenagers. I also remind *him* that teachers and parents will be reading this, too, so we'll try to strike a good compromise.

Now let's talk about *you*. Who would you like to be like—Thomas Edison, Martin Luther King, Jr., Steven Spielberg, Robin Williams, Gary Larson, Barbara Streisand, John F. Kennedy, Oprah Winfrey, Michael Jordan or some other great genius? How about learning to be the best *you* that you can be, and bring out your own inner genius? **EmpowerMind** will help you do just that.

Take your time while reading this book. Read it over and over again, but when you are asked to stop, and to follow certain directions, plans, or missions, do it right away. For example, do this now. Shut your eyes and count to ten. Did you do it? Good! When you are asked to do something before reading further—do it! Sounds easy, eh? It is. **EmpowerMind** is easy, if you don't fight it.

"Be cool. Listen to Kimberly and just go with it."

So, pull up a comfortable chair, a sofa, a pizza, a soda or whatever you need to keep your mind on the book and off your body, and *let the magic begin...*

You will begin every chapter by reading a few questions. You won't know the answers to most of these questions, but that's OK, read them anyway. *Why?* Because it will help you get the most out of this book. You want to discover your inborn genius, don't you?

"Hey, I know some of you have never read a book. Like, hey man, I know you think it's not cool; you'd rather be surfing, skating, or biking, dude! I understand, but this book's different. We've taken the torture out of reading—I think you'll like it."

The questions aren't in the front of the book to torture you. That comes later. (Just joking.) See, if you know what is expected from each chapter, you'll know what's important, and your mind will automatically look for it.

"We're talking no extra time or effort in reading, dude."

You see, your subconscious mind records everything, but I'll talk more about that later. For now, just remember that before reading on, answer the questions on the first page of each chapter, then answer the questions you find at the end of the chapter and compare your results. I'll bet you get more than 75% of the answers right after you have read it once. In **EmpowerMind** all you have to do is apply yourself, have fun doing it, and *you will see the results!* Good luck!

You're a Genius —

And I Can Prove It!

Discover How Easy Learning Can Be

Overview

In this first chapter you'll learn that association is the basis of all learning, and that without association you can learn nothing. You will learn why sometimes it is hard to learn, and sometimes it is easy. You will learn how to make learning easy. Would you like to learn to communicate better with people and have better relationships, too? Before finding out how, try to answer these questions.

Questions[*]

1. Association is the basis of *all*_____

2. Without association, we can learn _____

3. True or False? When we have a common association base with someone, then communication is usually easy. _____

4. Our association base is the same as our past_____

5. If our teachers or bosses teach us something and we just can't understand it, it probably means:
   A. We're stupid and should give up, so we don't embarrass ourselves.
   B. Our teacher or boss needs to talk *down* to our level.
   C. We are in our beta state of mind.
   D. Our teachers or bosses are not effective communicators.
   E. None of the above.

---

[*]   *Answers to all questions can be found at the back of the book.*

6. Give two examples of how you will practice what you have learned about association and its importance in learning. _____

_____

7. Give an example of how you can use your imagination to make learning or everyday life more fun. _____

_____

OK, you are ready now. You may read on.

Association is the basis of all learning. Without association, we can learn nothing. This is the core of the whole learning process and the **EmpowerMind** philosophy. It's been around for thousands of years; it just hasn't been the focus of learning like it should be. So, what does this mean? Learning is a series of building blocks, based on our past experiences. Association is exactly the same.

Think back to when you were three or four years old. Think of a time when you were playing and learning how to swing, build a castle, ride a bike, or learning anything. Shut your eyes and think about it.

Many students use words like happy, free, carefree, excited, peaceful and *fun* to describe their experience. Did you? If you did, too, then what happened to this attitude? What happened along the way that made learning tiresome, boring, exhausting and dreadful? Let's explore what happened to you—and how to get the joy of learning back again. Hang in there, this is an exciting adventure we are on together.

Now, shut your eyes and imagine an ice cream cone. Come on…shut your eyes and imagine an ice cream cone! Like the Nike ads say, "*Just do it!*"

What did your ice cream cone look like? Was it chocolate or strawberry? Was it sherbet or yogurt? Did it have a sugar cone or a regular cone? Even when a word like "ice cream" is presented to a group, the pictures are still all different. For instance, mine was chocolate and vanilla, with fudge chunks, caramel swirls, and nuts on a waffle cone. *See!* I bet yours was very different from mine. You see, everyone has different imaginations; therefore, it makes sense that we all have different association bases.

The same thing occurs with communication, following directions, and our perception of things. It's the same way when we first learn something. If someone tries to teach you something like 2 + 2 = 4, but you don't know what numbers are, you cannot learn. If someone tries to teach you to read, but letters look different in your eyes than theirs (for instance, a "b" looks like a "d" to you), then reading may be difficult. If someone tells you you can cook if you just follow the recipe, but you don't know what **"beating,"** **"separating,"** and **"simmering"** mean in *cooking language*, then you can't cook properly. I could fill a book with examples, but so could you. Take a moment and think of times when you didn't understand someone or something and *why* you didn't understand. It happens constantly. This is why it is important when we communicate, teach or learn, that we start from a common association base. Stop here and think about it.

In schools, teachers sometimes teach a "left-brain" style of learning, which is technical, analytical and unimaginative. The standard school's teaching style is usually effective for the left-brain learner. In fact, it's usually a piece of cake. If you are a *right*-brain learner, which means technical and analytical you are *not*, and you are *very* imaginative, then you may be labeled "learning disabled," "problem student," "special education student" or some other term. Labels are bad, because if you are labeled with this information about yourself, you might believe it. If school or specific subjects are difficult for you, it does *not* mean you are stupid. It *only* means you learn differently. Most students use both sides of their brains; one side is simply dominant over the other side. Both right- and left-brain learners are perfect. They simply have a unique style of learning. How could *that* be wrong, bad or stupid? You and I are going to discover how *you* learn

throughout this book. Once you discover your own process of learning, you will be able to learn from *your* association base and learning will become easy.

> # I know that you believe that you understand what you think I said, but I am not sure you realize that what you heard is not what I meant.
> —*Anonymous*

Have you ever felt as though you have explained something, and the person receiving the information didn't have a clue as to what you meant?

"Hmm...does this ever happen with...um...say, um...parents?"

This happens almost daily for some people (I'm included). We live in what I refer to as "*Association Bubbles.*" When someone says a word or a phrase, that same phrase may mean ten different things to ten different people; it all depends on their association base—their past experience. The only way you can transmit information, so it is understood, is to understand the person or people you are talking with. We each have a unique *association bubble.* When we can merge with another *association bubble* (another person) the magic of communication occurs.

You create your own reality in learning and in life via your natural and learned association base. You have the *power* to make choices about who you are and who you would like to become. Just because a teacher teaches in a way you cannot understand, doesn't mean the problem lies with *you.*

"Let me try to explain. Listen, dudes, let's say an alien comes down from outer space. (It's gross to the max.) Let's say you have just taught this alien all the basic words of the English language. Now, you, being the friendly polite dude you are, want to offer this alien food. All you know how to make is a peanut butter and jelly sandwich, but you can make it well! You get excited about teaching this alien how to make one for herself. (Hey, who said aliens were all males?) You want to see how good a teacher you really are. You instruct her with brilliance. (I mean, how hard is it to make a peanut butter and jelly sandwich?) Got the picture? OK, Kimberly, you take it from here."

You start by telling her to open the bag of bread. *She tears open the wrong side.* You realize she is taking you literally, so you modify.

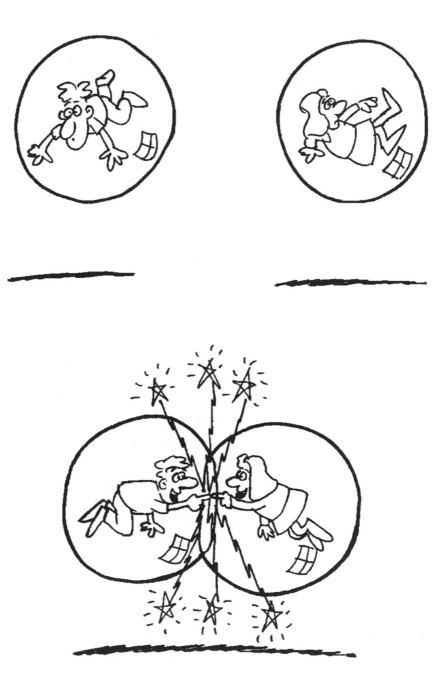

Your next instruction is to take out a piece of bread. (You're proud; you *know* she'll get this one.) *She pulls a piece off a slice of bread.* Oh, boy— you're in trouble now! With a smile on your face, you ask her to pull out a slice of bread and set it on the table in front of her. *She does it!* You're on a roll now! You now ask her to take off the peanut butter lid and scoop out some peanut butter. *She*

does it—with her hand! This is getting *very* messy. OK, now, you are going to get serious. You ask her to take the knife and put it in the peanut butter jar. *She does, but upside down.* You haven't given up yet. You ask her to pull out a big glob of peanut butter with the other end of the knife. *She pulls it out all right—and it flies across the room.* Now, frustration has set in. You ask her to put the peanut butter that's left on the knife onto the piece of bread. *She goes back into the bag and pulls out a small corner of a slice (a piece) and puts it on the bread.* I would have thought you would have learned by now. You screwed up the word "piece" before. You finally take the ingredients away from her and do it yourself!

Does this sound familiar? Does this exercise mean that *you* are stupid, because you couldn't teach the alien? Of course not! Does it mean that the alien was stupid? Of course not! It simply means that you had different association bases. This happens all the time. Try it with your friends or in your classroom. You become the alien, and they have to teach *you* how to make it. They can only give you one command at a time. It will create a lot of laughs and a lot of frustration. Or maybe you can use it for a speech in school on association. If you do, let me know your results. I love success stories! You can write to me at the following address: **EmpowerMind,** 38 Miller Avenue, Suite 201, Mill Valley, CA 94941.

The peanut butter and jelly sandwich example happens a lot. People tell me all the time that when someone is trying to show them how to do or learn something, the "teacher" often just gets frustrated and comes over and does it for them. They do this instead of teaching them how to work out the problem on their own. That's like giving someone fish instead of teaching him or her *how* to fish. Long term, it's just not as beneficial.

Now do you understand that you are *not* stupid if you don't understand something right away? You are like the alien in some subjects, and the teacher is like you were. Teaching is not easy. It is especially difficult if you are teaching from an association base that doesn't mean anything to the person you are teaching. You need to take responsibility for helping create common association bases with your teachers. Let your teachers know when your association base does not match theirs.

One of my former graduates, who truly understood the association base principles, continued to practice them with professors in college. She had an Abnormal Psychology class. She knew the material inside and out, but she couldn't take the teacher's multiple choice tests well. She could always see why another answer would work, too. So, she went to the teacher after the test and explained her situation. He asked her to explain why she chose the answers she did. She explained. He said he knew, now, that she did know the material. He just couldn't believe she could see the answers from "that perspective." On the back of all future tests, he let her explain the answers she chose. She got an A in the course. She would have had a C otherwise. Was she stupid or was he? *No! Neither one!* They just had different association bases. We cannot change the way all of our teachers teach, but we can try to build common association bases. You will learn about this throughout this book. If you can't learn from a teacher, talk to the teacher, in a very respectful way, of course. It really will help.

Think about your own life, when you get into an argument with someone. Doesn't it seem that if the story is repeated by you and the other person, the stories are very different? How about when you see a movie with a friend, when your friend likes it and you don't? Doesn't it seem like you each saw different movies? How about a party or a vacation? You have one story and your friends have a whole other version. It's not because the events, movies, conversations, etc. were different—it's because your association base is different from everyone else's. You create your own reality based on your past experiences.

There was a kindergarten teacher in one of my workshops. Her name was Marilyn and she had been an excellent teacher for 23 years. She started to tell me about one of her students. A boy she had in class could not tell which letters were which, and he didn't know the sounds of the letters. She tried giving him associations to remember; she tried games and music. She tried everything *but* creating a common association base that she had *him* develop. What I suggested she try was to have the boy (who she said had a GREAT imagination) make up pictures of what *he* thought the letters looked like. For instance the letter "B" looks like a bee (the actual bug) and makes a bzzzz sound. Well, she left and came back the next week with tremendous news. The kindergarten boy created pictures quickly and easily that reminded him of the sounds. He learned eight out of eight letters they practiced and got them all right.

Just because school is difficult or it takes you a long time to study, doesn't mean that you are stupid, it just means you learn differently. Our society puts emphasis on achievement based in reading, writing, and arithmetic. If you are great in art, music, physical education or special communication and relationship classes, you may receive a pass or fail grade. How can this make you feel, if you are a genius in these areas, and you only get a pass/fail grade or a satisfactory/unsatisfactory grade? Do you think Rembrandt or Steven Jobs (founder of Apple computer) needed to know how to dissect a frog? Do you think Beethoven needed to know how to do calculus? They are geniuses and so are you. Believe in your abilities and their importance, no matter *what* your school believes.

I'm *not* saying that reading, writing, and arithmetic aren't important. I'm saying do *not* discount the abilities you *do* have; they are just as important. *You*

are important! You have something very valuable to give this world, and you will find out what it is, if you haven't already.

All you need to do is find out *how you learn*, and all your learning will become easy. You see, the alphabet didn't change for the boy—just the way in which he learned it. This is the same for everyone. Our brains are all like computers, but they are infinitely more effective. The problem has been that we, as a society, have never been given "manuals" on how to use our brains. Therefore, when we have information put into our brain in the wrong way, it doesn't work properly. If IBM software were inserted into an Apple computer then there would not be an effective connection. This same result occurs when you are taught in a way in which you, as an individual, cannot receive the information. OK, let's look at it this way: If we are all IBM computers and we are being taught from an Apple manual, how can we learn properly? Well, from what I have discovered, we *can't!* What I would like to show you is a new path, a third alternative. This alternative deals with expanding your association base to connect to the person who you are learning from or with the person you are teaching. This can happen when you let go of expectations based only on your past experiences.

Let's say some friends tell you they have a surprise planned for you on your birthday. They seem to be excited. You are trying to guess what it is, but they won't give you any clues. You decide (create *"expectations"*) that it is a surprise party. You have always dreamed of having one and now it is going to happen. The big day comes and two of your friends pick you up in their car. (You are imagining all the friends awaiting you at the party.) They blind fold you (which is appropriate for a surprise party). You drive around awhile, and when you finally land at your destination — they remove the blindfold. You are standing in front of a collage of pictures that they had put together for you of all your fun times together. You anxiously look around. No more friends — *no* party. The disappointment must show in your face. Your birthday is a let down. The *only* reason it is, is because *you* had expectations that were *not* met, and you were disappointed. If you learn to open up your association base and lose your constant expectations, life can become a delightful and continuous surprise of spontaneous adventure.

Are you with me? OK, I still don't make sense? Try this. Think about a time when you did something spontaneously. Maybe you went on a spontaneous date or a spontaneous trip. Was it fun? Think about it.

I knew your answer would be *"yes,"* because when we live life spontaneously, we have no expectations. When we anticipate a date, a trip or anything, our expectations are generally so great that we lose the magic in the moment. You see, we create something in our minds a certain way, and then our expectations aren't fulfilled. Think about all the times in your life when you have been spontaneous versus when you have planned, calculated, or expected something. You decide which has been more enjoyable. If you haven't been spontaneous, then that's your first lesson. *Be more spontaneous! Live life in the moment, without expectation, and truly the magic will begin!*

How does this all continue to pertain to learning? *Good question.* Before I tell you, let me show you another example. Look closely at the pictures on the next two pages, and answer the following question about each of them. Do it to the best of your ability. Which one is a (*note:* some may be two of these and some may be none of these):

1. Mail clerk
2. Bus driver
3. Entrepreneur
4. High school principal
5. Marketer/Salesperson
6. Film maker
7. Businessman
8. Environmentalist
9. Psychologist
10. Chef
11. Minister
12. Visionary
13. Artist
14. Boatman

1

2

_____

_____

_____

_____

3

4

_____

_____

_____

_____

Now turn to page 24 and check your answers.

So, how did you do? I certainly wouldn't even expect you to be close because *nobody* should know what a person is all about based on a picture, or even a first introduction. So…why this exercise? To see what biases and prejudices you have (which we *all* have in one way or another) based on your own association bases. We cannot judge someone and we cannot define someone based on our limited experience—our limited association base. It is amazing to me how quickly we, as a society, judge other people with as little information as physical appearance. I *know* I still do this sometimes. If you are aware that you do this, then you are headed in the right direction, because when we are aware of our issues, we can start to change them.

I remember when I was in college. My best friend, Sheila, was telling me that her roommate hugged her mother when she came to visit. She assumed that they were lesbians. She assumed this because she had such little affection in her own family and from her own mother. She interpreted the reality of the situation based *only* on her past experience. How many times do you do this? How many times do you think you have distorted the truth? Stop *right now* and think about this.

You are learning *all* the time, it doesn't *always* have to be associated with schools. You learn everyday. Don't limit your definition of learning. Before you move into the next chapter and learn some of the basics about how *your* brain operates, I'd like to share with you some of the *Greats* who were considered learning disabled, stupid, slow learners and problem students. Think about what

your label is, created by your peers, not by yourself and ask yourself, "Is that *really* me?" Steven Spielberg said he was considered learning disabled and feels like every film may be a failure and he's nervous for work every day. *Why?* Because he was "learning disabled." Edison and Einstein were considered kooks in school. They were "crazy" and look what they accomplished! Spud Webb is 5'7" and won the slam-dunk contest in professional basketball. Do you think he was told or taught he would be truly great? How about Tom Cruise and Cher, who are both dyslexics? They were "learning problem" children. You may be one of these greats. I'll put odds on it that you are.

We all have an inner genius in us, waiting to be encouraged to come out. You may not be getting any support from the outside world, but it doesn't mean that your inner genius doesn't exist. It surely exists. *You* need to believe it and program your computer with *"I can do it"* thoughts, instead of "I can't, shouldn't, or won't be able to" thoughts. We will spend a whole chapter on programming later, but until you get there you need to know that real limitations exist *only* in your mind. Like a computer, you can program your brain to achieve, believe, and succeed.

If you would like to learn how your brain works and how to make *all* learning easy by discovering how your brain works, then read on. You'll be amazed at what you will discover you can do.

All right, let's look at something that *seems* to be common to most people. Are *you* great at remembering people's names? Hmm…I didn't think so. What would you think if *you* could learn a simple way to remember people's names?

Pretty great, eh? Well, believe it, because you will. Rule number one in this book and in your mind must be, "I believe I can do it and I will practice, practice, practice, practice, practice!" If you really want to impress a person or group of people, learn how to learn names. People will be sure you are a genius, because so few people do this effectively. It's a great way to make an excellent impression on new friends or work associates.

First, we will look at our menu of techniques. The word "Menu" is used, because everyone learns differently so you will get lots of choices. You can use a combination of these choices, one of the choices, or all of them; in fact, maybe you even have one that is not here that works for you. If that is true—*great!* It is most important that you work with what works for you, stick with it, and improve upon it.

So, here's the menu:

> **E — Engrain** the name in your mind
> **M — Mention** the name verbally and non-verbally
> **P — Play** with the name
> **O — Overplay** the name in your mind
> **W — Wait** for an association to the name
> **E — Exaggerate** the name and picture it
> **R — Repeat** the name after you leave the person(s)

What does all of this mean? Good question. Let's begin with the first technique. **E — ENGRAIN** the name in your mind. Engrain means to really hear it, concentrate on it, and *don't* let the person continue talking until you have heard his or her name. If you haven't heard it properly the first time then:

1. Don't ask again; they'll think you're stupid
2. Grab a piece of paper and write it down as they are talking.
3. Ask them to repeat it and maybe even spell it for you.

Yes! You guessed it! The answer is the third one. You see, a person's name, to that person, is the most important sound s/he could hear in any language. The person will be honored and feel like you care about him or her if you ask him or her to repeat it.

The second technique is you should **M — MENTION IT.** After the person introduces him or herself, repeat the name yourself. You could say, "It's nice to meet you, Wilbur." Or, "Hey, Wilbur, dude, rad name." You can also repeat the name in your head silently. This really helps you engrain it deeper and helps make it stick.

The third technique is to **P — PLAY WITH IT.** This means you can make Wilbur into a cartoon character, or a giant, or any other outrageous thing he reminds you of, at that moment. It is important that this image reflects his name in some way.

The fourth technique is **O — OVERPLAY IT.** This means to say the name in your mind over and over again. This does *not* and I repeat, does *not* mean say it out loud over and over again. Have you ever met the stereotypical sales person who says, "Oh, it's nice to meet you, John. So, John, where are you from? Ah, Idaho, John! Well, John, Idaho is a nice place to be from. So, John how long have you been out here? Ah, two years John..." When I say *overplay it*, I mean in your head, as the day or evening progresses. If you are in school, at a party, at a work function, etc., keep overplaying all the people in your mind, throughout the evening, to make sure you remember *all* of their names. If you forget one or two, ask someone else their names, and then continue overplaying them. Try to look at their faces, or at least picture their faces in your mind, as you say their names. This will help you remember them all night and most of them for a while after.

The fifth technique is **W — WAIT FOR AN ASSOCIATION.** Why should you wait? This is important, because many times an association doesn't emerge. If it doesn't come to you quickly, *forget it*. If you try too hard, you will be focusing so much on the association that you'll miss what the person is saying and *that* will be more embarrassing than forgetting the person's name! For example, Denise St. Dennis was one of my students. Immediately, I thought of "she falls on 'de knees' and prays to St. Dennis." It worked and it stuck. But—you may get a name like Amori Kuzpetulenx—and you can't even pronounce it, much less associate it with an image. If you can think of an association to the name right away, *great!* If not, *great!* This is just a menu. *You* decide what works for *you*.

The sixth technique is **E — EXAGGERATE IT**. This means make the name colorful, big, outrageous, or funny. The more you exaggerate, the more zany it is, the easier it will be to remember. I was having the hardest time remembering the pronunciation of a new friend's name; it was spelled Lourdes. It was pronounced "*lord-es*." I imagined her being a lord. (She looked like a goddess, so it was easy for me.) Then I imagined a snake shaped like an "S" across her body. So, when I saw her, I naturally thought of Lord-S. I have another friend named Addrell. Many people, including myself, had a hard time with his name, so I imagined "*a drill*" going through his head. I made it big, too. *A drill* was my trigger for Addrell. It worked for me and for other people who had a hard time with his name. This is a fun one to do. In fact, if your name is hard to remember, give other people a funny exaggerated picture to help them remember it.

The last, and often the most important technique, is **R — REPEAT IT**. This is only if you want to learn the names long term. If you only need to learn names for an evening, do not use this one. There is no sense in using another technique, if it won't benefit you in some way. Use the long term technique only when you need to really remember names over a period of time. When you go home after meeting the person, think of the person's face and attach his or her name to the person or vice-versa. Do this the first few nights before you go to bed; then once a week, then once a month—until it is stuck in your conscious mind. This will really impress (it will astound, amaze, flabbergast) the person when you remember his or her name a long time later.

Now, write down when you will use this within the next week.

_____

_____

Then, test yourself when you get home after the event. I think you will be amazed at your success. You *must* practice right away, so you will see how well you do. It will raise your confidence and your self-esteem. Besides, then you will *know* that all this stuff I'm writing about really *does work*.

A student named Joe used this technique at a wedding. He learned more than fifty names. That in itself is awesome, but these were Indian names. They were *tough* for him to learn, because they were foreign to his association base. They were also hard names to pronounce. He repeated the names and had the people spell them for him. He made associations with the names, exaggerated them and repeated them to himself over and over again. He not only remembered them, but he pronounced them correctly. The people were amazed and complimented him. He really made them feel important. They were so impressed by him because everyone always forgot or at least mispronounced their names. Joe was flying with excitement! Oh, by the way, Joe said when entering the course (before using this menu of techniques) that he could *never* remember anyone's name, even right after first meeting them. Joe says, if he can do it, *so can you!* I believe him. So, *just do it!*

Think of all those fine guys and girls whose names you *want* to remember, and how impressed they will be when you can easily remember *all* of their names. It impresses other people because a person's name, to that person, is the sweetest and most important sound in any language. This alone will help make you a hit at parties and in school.

If you get in touch with how your own computer—your brain—works, then learning will become easy. Try it and believe in yourself. *You can do anything!*

Summary

Learning to learn becomes easy when you realize that all you need is an association base to learn. You interpret the world around you based *only* on your own experience. You create your own reality, based on past experience. When you create common associations, you create common communication; thus creating common learning bases. *Association is the basis of all learning.*

Questions

1. Association is the basis of *all*_____

2. Without association, we can learn _____

3. True or False? When we have a common association base with someone, then communication is usually easy. _____

4. Our association base is the same as our past_____

5. If our teachers or bosses teach us something and we just can't understand it, it probably means:
    A. We're stupid and should give up, so we don't embarrass ourselves.
    B. Our teacher or boss needs to talk *down* to our level.
    C. We are in our beta state of mind.
    D. Our teachers or bosses are not effective communicators.
    E. None of the above

6. Give two examples of how you will practice what you have learned about association and its importance in learning. _____
    _____

7. Give an example of how you can use your imagination to make learning or everyday life more fun._____
    _____

8. In this chapter, EMPOWER is a trigger for:
    A. The name of this book
    B. The menu to remember names
    C. A gun
    D. All of the above

9. EMPOWER stands for:
    E: _____
    M: _____
    P: _____
    O: _____
    W: _____
    E: _____
    R: _____

10. One of the major goals of this chapter was to:
    A. Learn how important it is to expand our association base.
    B. Learn that if our teachers learned to teach, we wouldn't have any learning problems.
    C. If we learned to communicate properly all our problems would disappear.
    D. Both A & C

11. A person's name, to that person, is the most important sound in any _____ .

Photo I.D.

1. Minister
2. Marketer/Salesperson
3. Minister
4. Film maker
5. Boatman/Businessman
6. Environmentalist/artist

Chapter Two

Learn to Memorize and Retain Anything

Overview

Your brain is like a computer, except it is much more powerful. Would you like to be able to use your computer effectively to memorize vocabulary, spelling words, lists of things, foreign languages and just about anything in a few minutes, and be able to remember it for as long as you want? If your answer is "*Yes,*" great, because this chapter is going to make learning names seem like kindergarten.

Questions

1. We automatically think in _____ .

2. We use less than (choose the closest answer):
   A. 50% of our brains
   B. 90% of our brains
   C. 25% of our brains
   D. We don't use our brains, they use us.
   E. 10% of our brains

3. Our imagination is:
   A. Limitless
   B. Controlled by our parents
   C. Limited to our personal experience
   D. Both B and C

4. True or False? Our imaginations are different from people in other parts of the world, but they are the same as citizens in the United States. _____

5. What is the best way to remember a list of twenty objects?
    A. You can't, your mind has limits.
    B. By cheating
    C. By making pictures out of the objects, then connecting those pictures.
    D. By repeating them over and over again, and having someone give you money, to give you incentive.

6. This helps us remember our words:
    A. Exaggeration
    B. Color
    C. Making them bizarre
    D. All of the above

7. Can we use imagery to learn vocabulary words? _____

    If so, how? _____

    _____

Our brains are like computers, only they are hundreds of times more powerful and effective. We have over one hundred billion brain cells, and we don't even use one tenth of the brain cells we have. Most people use less than 10% of their brain. What would happen if you only used 10% of your arms or legs? Well, it's the same with the brain. You need to learn how it works, in order to use it properly. The next two chapters will teach you that. You are crawling now, but after this chapter, you will be ready to take your first step. So, let's just jump right into it. Shut your eyes and think of an alien.

> "Hey! Did you do it? It's cool when you follow Kimberly's directions. It makes sense once you try it. Remember, I know how you may feel. I was one of her greatest rebels, before I knew better. My advice is just do it!"

OK now, was your alien green? Gray? Fat? Short? Bald? Toothless? Did it have antennas? Or, was it completely different? I'll bet it was different, because you have a unique imagination. It is different from anyone else's imagination in the world, and that is what makes you so special! So, you know that not only do you have a unique imagination, but you also know that you *think* in pictures. You did not see the letters A-L-I-E-N, did you? You actually saw the alien in a picture. You created what you wanted. You cannot only make a picture, but you can exaggerate it, make it big, small, dark light or whatever you choose. If you didn't see a picture that is OK You may have heard an alien sound, or you may have smelled an alien. You may have made the sound, loud or soft, buzzing or smooth. You may have smelled a sharp odor or a bland odor; whatever you experienced is

perfect. Continue the exercise replacing the pictures with sounds, smells, colors or whatever works for you. (Do this only if you did not see pictures.) **Your imagination is *limitless!***

Now, shut your eyes again and think of the word *"fun"* and what it means to you.

Well, what did you see? I bet you saw some picture that reminded you of "fun." I bet your picture was different from mine, because (think back to chapter one) you have a different association base, based on your past experience.

Now, shut your eyes and think of the word "success."

See, **you can picture anything in your mind.** No matter what word you give yourself, you will be able to picture it. Try it with some more words.

1. Frustration
2. Happiness
3. Boring
4. Fast
5. Disgusting

How did you do? My bet is that you had some great pictures. Now that you know you think in images and pictures, and that you can picture anything, you know the basic lesson of how your brain works.

Now let's see what else it can do. How long would it take you to memorize twenty objects in a row? Well, if you said more than five to ten minutes, you will be in for a pleasant surprise. As you look at each word, you must imagine (get a visual picture of) each item. Then, you must link them together (**only two at a time**). Remember, your imagination is limitless, so exaggerate, make the pictures colorful and above all have fun!

Here are the twenty objects you are going to memorize:

1. Ice cream cone	8. Flowers	15. Sunglasses
2. Skunk	9. Fork	16. Finger
3. Teacher	10. Belly button	17. Lamp
4. Heart	11. Worm	18. Hamburger
5. Balloon	12. Kite	19. Mickey Mouse
6. Nail	13. Horse	20. Skateboard
7. Hand	14. High heels	

OK, are you ready to be awesome? Are you ready to amaze even yourself? Now, before you go on, you have to make me a promise. If you learn how to memorize at least fifteen of these in ten minutes or less (and remember all of them for at least a week) then you have to commit to continuing reading this book with an open mind, and an attitude that you can do anything! Is that a deal? I hope so. Don't let me down. Better yet, don't let yourself down.

OK, I want you to close your eyes and imagine the following pictures in your mind (do it *slowly*):

(1) A huge scoop of *"ice-cream"* (at least fifty feet high). Climbing out of this huge scoop of ice-cream is a (2) long skinny *"skunk."* The skunk's spraying its smelly spray all over (3) your favorite *"teacher."* Your teacher's (4) *"heart"* is so big, caring and light that it floats up in the air like a big (5) *"balloon."* As the balloon floats up, you notice (6) a huge sixty-foot *"nail"* flying down and popping it.

Now, let's repeat those together. You started with a fifty foot _____. A _____ crawled out of it and squirted your favorite _____ who had a big, huge, caring _____ that turned into a _____ and then a _____ came flying down.

Now, let's try it without looking at the clues.

1._____   4._____

2._____   5._____

3._____   6._____

Are you good or what?! Let's keep going. You can even keep your eyes open if you want. Let's see how good you really are.

The nail is being pounded through (7) your *"hand."* Instead of blood gushing out you see (8) *"flowers"* growing. In the middle of the flowers there is a (9) *"fork."* growing. The fork was stabbed into a (10) *"belly button."*

Now, let's do it again.

You started with a fifty foot _____. A _____ crawled out of it and squirted _____ who had a big, huge, caring_____ that turned into a _____ and then a _____ came flying down into your _____. Instead of blood there was a _____growing.

In the middle of the flowers there was a _____ growing. It was stabbed into a _____.

Let's go again…

Yahoo!! You're halfway there! Don't give up now. If you got half of the 10 right you're doing great, and better than you would have before. So, stick with me, we're going all the way this time.

Out of the belly button crawled a (11) *"worm."* The worm didn't turn into a butterfly, it turned into a (12) *"kite,"* and the kite was being flown by a (13) *"horse"* wearing (14) *"high heels."* These high heels came smashing down on a pair of very tiny (15) *"sunglasses."* The sunglasses were disgusting, because there was a (16) *"finger"* sticking out of one of the lenses. The finger was burned because it got stuck in a (17) *"lamp."* The lamp was made of smelly (18) *"hamburger."* Who was eating the hamburger you ask? (19) *"Mickey Mouse,"* of course. And, Mickey Mouse was skating like a pro on a (20) *"skateboard."*

You're done! Let's see how you'll do.

You started with a fifty foot _____. A _____ crawled out of it and squirted _____ who had a big, huge, caring _____ that turned into a _____. And then a _____ came flying down into your _____. Instead of blood there were _____ growing. In the middle of the flowers there was a _____ growing. It was stuck in a _____ There was a _____ crawling out of it and it turned into a _____. A _____ started flying it, and the thing flying it was wearing _____. Then these things it was wearing broke a pair of _____ that had a _____ growing out of them. It got burned in a _____. That was made of _____, which was eaten by _____. This thing was skating on a _____.

Ta-Da! You are done! Let's see if you can get them without the clues. Give it a try.

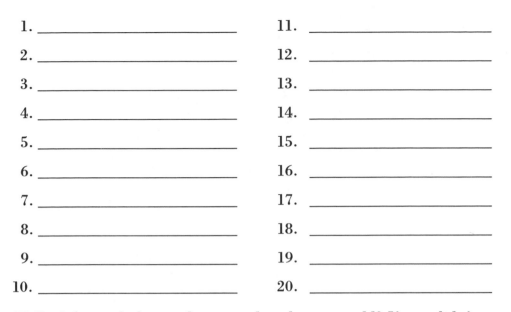

Well, did you do better than you thought you could? If you didn't get all twenty, that's OK. Go back and review it again. I'm sure you'll get it after just a little more practice. Isn't it amazing how easy it is when you picture them?

Another rule is that our mind likes to think of as few things at a time as possible. That is why, when you use this picturing technique, **you only need to attach two objects at a time.** You need to let go of the object before the object you are currently picturing. It is easy for us to learn one thing at a time (like learning the alphabet one letter at a time). But, if we try to learn too much at once, our brain freaks out, and we feel overwhelmed by too much information (like, if we had to learn all 26 letters in the alphabet at once).

What am I talking about? Well, it's time for an example. When I had you picture ice-cream, and then a skunk coming out of it, you dropped the ice-cream and just noticed what the skunk was doing (which was spraying the teacher). Then you lost the picture of the skunk and just saw what was happening to the teacher. The whole list went like that. It would have been too hard if you had to remember all twenty at a time, but two at a time is easy! That's the way our brain likes to work. It *loves* to simplify things.

So, you used my imagination, which is harder for you believe me. Now, it's your turn to make it easier, and use your own imagination. It will be easier, but remember a few helpful hints:

1. **Our mind remembers pictures better when they are colorful and exaggerated.**
2. **The more bizarre and strange, the easier they will be to remember.**

So, exaggerate them, make them colorful and bizarre. Well, try it for yourself. Work with these ten objects and see how you do. Remember, attach two at a time.

1. Television
2. Pig
3. Knife
4. Watermelon
5. Toilet

6. Dog
7. Taxicab
8. Tree
9. Book
10. Banana

Did you attach only two pictures at a time? First, the television and the pig, then the pig and the knife, then the knife and the watermelon, etc. Sometimes, I just ask myself the question, "What's going on with the word?" What's going on with the television; then, what's going on with the pig; then what's going on with the knife, etc. That may also work for you. *You can do it!*

I'm so excited that you are learning this. This exercise alone will open up all sorts of possibilities for you. Just keep practicing until you can have someone give you a list of twenty objects and you can recite all of them back. Once you are able to do this, it is time to read on and see the other ways you can apply what you have learned. Practice this before reading further.

Take this a step further. Let's try vocabulary. Put on your imagination cap, because you are really going to need it on this one!

Let's look at the word, *"furibund."*

What does it remind you of in a word or a few words that you already know? Write it down. _____

_____

Separate the word, if you need to separate it. Furi Bund.

Think of the words that remind you of that. I thought of a furry band. Then, I made a picture of it. I want you to do the same. If furry band works, use it. If you have a better word or words, then use yours.

Now, you have a picture. My picture is of a furry band.

FURIBUND = FURRY BAND = FURIOUS

Next, you attach the meaning of the word to the picture. The meaning of furibund is "rage or furious." So attach this meaning (the picture of) rage or furious.

For example, I saw my "furry band" with a big mouth screaming with rage. When I see the word furibund, I ask myself, "What does that remind me of? Ah ha! A furry band." Then I ask myself, "What is going on with the furry band? Ah ha! It is screaming with rage!" There's my answer and it's easy to remember. I want you to ask yourself the same questions, and do the same thing I just did.

Now, it's time for you to practice. Try doing this with the following words:

Eburnation. What picture do you get from this word? What does it remind you of? Either write it or draw it.

_____

_____

_____

_____

Eburnation means *"an abnormal condition in which bones become hard and dense."* Now, attach its meaning to your picture.

_____

_____

_____

Do the same with the following. Attach the picture that reminds you of the word, with the picture that reminds you of the definition. Re-read the example with furry band if you are confused.

Catechin means "a yellow compound."

_____

_____

_____

Aitchbone means "the cut of beef that includes this bone."

_____

_____

_____

Mutable means "constantly changing."

_____

_____

_____

MUTABLE = MOO TABLE = CHANGEABLE

When I said make things colorful, exaggerate them and make them bizarre, I meant it.

"I remember when I was given the French word 'piscine.' It sounds like pits zeen. I made the easiest association, and it just made me laugh..."

Wait! Hacker, I said to keep those associations to yourself. That is the rule, even though I agree that it was your easiest association ever. Associations can be bizarre and even off-color, but if they are keep them to yourself. We'll start with another bizarre, yet more appropriate example, than that last one.

The word is *gastrocnemius*. It means "calf muscle." One student said "gastroc" sounded like a gas truck, another said nemius reminded her of Nieman Marcus. A third student put the picture together. She had a gas truck going to Neiman Marcus. Then, as I recall, Hacker had the gas truck hit a calf (the animal) on its way to Nieman Marcus. He made it pretty gory, so I'll leave out the details.

Half the class was grossed out, but they all remembered it.

Remember, this is your very own secret and personal system. Nobody has to know it but you! If gory and sick work for you then use them, just remember...don't share them with others.

Try this system with your vocabulary words in school. It works the same exact way with foreign languages. If you are having a hard time understanding this, or you can't think of a picture, then work with someone else. Show someone else the book and practice with him or her. Don't ever try to handle things that are confusing and difficult by yourself. There are always people who can help you. Plus, don't expect yourself to be perfect at this yet. You will improve with practice.

Hacker, you use this method a lot don't you?

"This way of memorizing is a riot to practice with friends 'cuz you have more crazy (and sometimes a little sick and gross) imaginations working together. Sometimes I just laugh through my tests when remembering my associations."

A thirteen year old student, Angela, used this principle and changed from D's on tests to A's. She was sold! You will be too, but you need to practice. In fact, Angela asked to go a step further. She asked me, "How can I use this for spelling?" I said, "Good question. Let's check it out." I looked at her spelling list and asked her, "What is the problem?" She said that she couldn't remember if there are two R's, two S's, two T's etc. in the words. So, we looked at a few of her words.

Benefited	Controlling
Scuffling	Bedding

Well, we looked at the word benefited and I asked her what she saw in the word that reminded her of something. She saw "*Ben getting fit. He was on a bike, and he was shaped like a tee. It was also a bike for 'one.'* "

This picture reminded her of Ben only being one "T" on the bike; therefore, benefited has only one "T."

Controlling reminded her of "*troll.*" The troll was a Siamese twin; therefore, controlling has two "L's."

Scuffling reminded her of "*skuff,*" which reminded her of shoes getting scuffs on them. Well, it's natural to think of two shoes together; therefore, scuffling has two "F's."

Bedding, naturally reminds her of "*bed.*" She thought of two pillows on a bed; therefore, it reminds her of two "D's" in bedding.

Why don't you try some on your own? You can do this with any spelling. Some people have a hard time remembering if words end in "ery" or "ary." One of my students suggested they think of "ery" as the word being "eerie" and "ary" as the word being "airy." Take for instance the word, *secretary* you could think of the secretary as being an air head. Or, for the word misery you can think of misery being *very* eerie. There are *no* rules. In EmpowerMind, you make them up. If it works, use it; however, I caution you not to share any stereotypic associations or any associations that may be offensive to someone. These associations are your secret and you don't want to hurt anyone.

Now, try it with the following words. But first, remember to look for a word or a trigger within the word, that will remind you of the spelling. If you have a hard time, re-read the above examples.

Epitome	Dessert
Fulfilling	Intrigue
Hors d'oeuvre	Principal

If these words were too easy, try it with words you have a hard time spelling.

How can you use this for math? That is a good question! You can use it to remember formulas and equations.

Let's say you have to memorize the quadratic formula $-b \pm \dfrac{\sqrt{b^2 - 4ac}}{2a}$.

Let's see how you could picture this. Shut your eyes and try it.

"That's too hard right now. Give them some examples before you plunge into a difficult mind blowing exercise. Haven't I heard someone say something like 'Walk before you run'?"

OK, I'll back up. I guess I was trying to teach you like the students tried to teach the alien. I assumed too much!

Let's try again. Numbers don't have to be pictured as numbers, but rather as things that remind us of numbers. Everyone will have something different, because we all have different association bases. A "4" may remind you of someone yelling "fore" at a golf course. It may remind you of a chair, because it has four legs or because it looks like an upside down chair. A "9" may remind you of a tadpole, a balloon with string, or a 9-hole golf course. Or you may just look at numbers and simply remember them by sight. If that's the case don't even try the picturing method. Remember, this book has menus of ideas. You have the choice of what you want or don't want to use. The choice is up to you.

Now, back to the quadratic equation. I'll make a picture first. This is how I see it.

You have a rope (*"minus"*) with a bee (*"b"*) dangling from it, buzzing around a cross (*"plus"*) that's stuck in a thin platform (*"minus"*). This cross, with the platform, is crashing into a gutter or a water drain (*"square root of"*). In the drain, is a bee in a square box (*"b squared"*). A rope is attached to the box (*"minus"*), hanging from this rope are 4 AC spark plugs (*"4ac"*). All of this is sitting on top of two apples. (*"This is all over 2a."*) Whew! It's a mouthful, but it's a lot easier to learn and retain the formulas when you learn them this way. You need to make up picture connections that work for you. Remember to attach two pictures at a time.

Another example is with fractions. Let's look at $\frac{1}{8}$ = .125.

It reminds me of "I/ate" "a dozen and a half of a donut." Stop and think about how I came up with that example.

Now you think of one. _____

Now try $\frac{1}{4}$ = .25

This reminds me of 1 chair (always has four legs), with a quarter ($.25) sitting on top of it. Now, you think of one.

_____

If you think it's difficult now, it's only because you need a little practice stretching your imagination. But I know you can do it! Remember, your imagination is limitless, and you can picture anything.

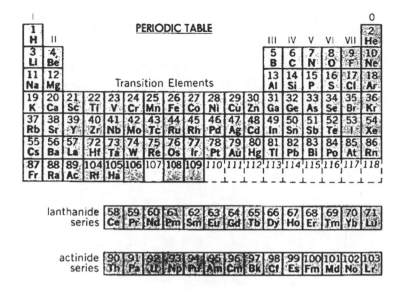

I'm going to challenge you now. How can you memorize the periodic table in science class? Look at these examples and you figure it out.

Let's assume that you have to learn the "inert gases." Simply create words that have the first two letters of these letter symbols for those gases. After you do this, make up a story and presto your inner genius has done it again! Oh! What's that, Hacker? You'd like me to do this for all of you? OK, I will this time, but you have to get used to doing this for yourself. These techniques are only as good as you make them with your imagination.

The words are: he, never, argues, kryptonite, Xerox, R.N. ("registered nurse"). The story: He never argues over kryptonite, while Xeroxing in front of the R.N.

HE NEVER ARGUES ABOUT KRYPTONITE
WHILE XEROXING WITH AN R.N.

You can learn this chart in several different ways. I prefer the combination method. (That is, anything that works!) You see the cartoon that shows the "NE" lit up like a neon sign? Well, you could also picture a "knee on" something, and the "knee" could be neon. For AL (aluminum), you may imagine a person you know named Al eating an aluminum can. You see, there are limitless ways to remember this chart (or anything for that matter). It is just up to you and your imagination (and how you think the teacher is going to test you), to make it all E.Z. (*easy* of course!)

It's really important that you try these techniques immediately! Use them to remember lists of things on your next vocabulary, foreign language, or spelling test.

If you practice right away, you will be reinforced and you will want to do it again and again. Think of how you will feel if you start getting A's on your tests, and you are only spending half the time you used to studying.

Don't forget to practice with friends. Share these techniques and this book, so they can learn how to make it easy, too. This way you can all perform well on your tests and make it fun studying together.

You can take this a step further and use it to remember scripts, poems, songs, anthems, Bible verses, and so on. How?

Well, you just picture the words. Unfortunately, we are taught in school to just repeat words over and over again verbally. When we learn poems we learn to say, "Mary had a little lamb. Its fleece was white as snow, and everywhere that Mary went, her lamb was sure to go. Mary had a little lamb. Its fleece was white as snow, and everywhere that Mary went, her lamb was sure to go. Mary had a little lamb. Its fleece was white as snow, and everywhere that Mary went, her lamb was sure to go. Mary had a little lamb. Its fleece was white as snow, and everywhere that Mary went, her lamb was sure to go." We say this over and over until we get it, or pass out from exhaustion.

Wouldn't it be easier and more fun to "imagine" Mary, she has a little lamb (*see it*) and everywhere that Mary went (*see Mary, see her going*) her lamb (*see it again*) was sure to go? If you visualize it, and see it as it is being said, it makes it real and a lot more fun—and ten times easier to learn and retain! I have had students learn four paragraphs word for word in about twenty minutes, and retain most of it. They have to practice it every so often, but it's a heck of a lot more effective than the other way, the hard way.

If you want to spend little to no time studying for your final exams, then definitely use this technique. You see, our minds remember in pictures better. If you review your words once a week, quickly (5-10 minutes maximum), you will remember almost all of them come final exam time. If you don't review any of them you'll still remember a great majority. The mind retains information in pictures much easier than in words.

Just do it!

Summary

Your imagination is limitless! Your mind can memorize anything by converting the information into pictures. You can visualize anything, even numbers and abstract words. The more you practice, the better you will become. You will remember information much longer by picturing it in your mind, because your mind automatically thinks in pictures.

Questions

1. We automatically think in _____ .

2. We use less than (choose the closest answer):
    A. 50% of our brains
    B. 90% of our brains
    C. 25% of our brains
    D. We don't use our brains, they use us.
    E. 10% of our brains.

3. Our imagination is:
    A. Limitless
    B. Controlled by our parents
    C. Limited to our personal experience
    D. Both B and C

4. True or False? Your imagination is different from the imaginations of people in other parts of the world, but it's the same as citizens in the United States.

5. What is the best way to remember a list of twenty objects and remember it?
   A. You can't, your mind has limits.
   B. By cheating
   C. By making pictures out of the objects, then connecting those pictures
   D. By repeating them over and over again, and having someone give you money, to give you incentive.

6. This helps us remember words:
   A. Exaggeration
   B. Color
   C. Making them bizarre
   D. All of the above

7. Can we use imagery to learn vocabulary words? _____
   If so, how?_____

8. Can we make pictures out of numbers? _____
   If you can, try it.

9. How might you remember to spell *"Controlling"*?

   _____

   _____

10. When we learn things in pictures it takes us:
    A. Exactly ten minutes to learn them
    B. Less time to learn them than before
    C. Only a few review sessions to retain them for months
    D. Both B and C

11. Our minds prefer to think:
    A. Of one to two things at a time
    B. As seldom as possible
    C. Of as much as possible, all at once
    D. Of cartoons most of the time
    E. Of a list of twenty items at a time

Chapter Three

> "You tell me, and I forget.
> You teach me, and I remember.
> You involve me, and I learn."
>
> — *Benjamin Franklin*

"How Do You Learn?"

Overview

Have you ever had a hard time remembering what a speaker has said? Has it been impossible for you to listen to a boring speaker and keep your attention focused? Is it sometimes hard for you to keep your focus and concentration? Have you ever had a hard time memorizing lists? Well, if you have answered yes to any of these questions, then you will love reading on. This chapter shows you how to make all these frustrations easier and more fun. It finally demonstrates what the word "trigger" means. It shows you how to use triggers in all learning situations, by using any or all of your six senses. Go for it!

Questions

1. One way to concentrate is to:
    A. Talk along with the speaker.
    B. Make pictures in your mind of what the speaker is saying.
    C. Ask the person next to you if s/he is hearing the same thing you are hearing.
    D. Don't do anything but study.

2. We think _____ as fast as we talk.
    A. Twice
    B. Almost twenty times
    C. Almost ten times
    D. Four times

3. What does mimicking mean? _____

_____

4. Triggers are: (Choose the best answer.)
    A. Letters
    B. Numbers
    C. Cheat-sheets
    D. Anything that reminds you of something
    E. None of the above

5. True or False? You can use triggers for all learning. _____

6. Triggers also help us: _____
    A. Retain information longer.
    B. Have fun while learning
    C. Make learning easy
    D. All of the above

Focusing

Let's begin with focusing and concentration. Write down three things that make you lose concentration when you listen to a speaker, lecturer, or teacher.

1. _____

2. _____

3. _____

Now re-read these three things, because I am going to see if I can answer for you how to eliminate all three of them.

Many times when we are listening to someone else speak, especially if they are boring, we tune out because: we have our mind on something else, we are bored, we are anxious, or we don't understand a word of what the speaker is saying. Isn't that a bummer after spending your money or your precious time?

So, how can you make listening easy and fun? I have some suggestions, but first I want you to know a few simple facts.

> **As fast as we talk, we listen almost three times faster.**
>
> **As fast as we talk, we think almost ten times faster.**
>
> **So we think more than twice as fast as we listen.**

Therefore, you are usually thinking way ahead of someone, even if s/he is a fascinating speaker. That's why what we often think we heard may not be what someone actually said. So, imagine where your thoughts might wander when the speakers are dull. Our minds are anywhere but on the speaker.

So, what can you do? Well, remember in elementary school when kids would mimic each other while they were talking? It was real annoying and incredibly immature. Well, that is what I would like you to do: *mimic mimic mimic!* But, there is one catch to it all. You have to do this in your head, *not* out loud. Do you know what I mean by the word "mimic"? Mimic means "copy." So, in this instance, I'd like you to talk at the same time the other person is talking. If you can think so much faster than someone is speaking, then it makes sense that you can speak at the same time as that person. Think about how many times you have wanted to, or that you have finished sentences for other people. Stop and think about what you just read. Now, go see that it's possible.

It's time to test it out. Next time you're talking with someone, one-on-one, look at the person's lips and repeat, in your mind—at the same time the person's talking—the words being said. You will be amazed at how easy it is to do this and how much easier you will stay present with the conversation. After you have practiced one-on-one, try it with a speaker, teacher, lecturer or a *loooong*-winded minister or rabbi. You will retain a great deal more information than you could have otherwise. It helps you keep your concentration.

Now, at the same time, you need to stay focused on the subject without losing concentration. You can do this and have a high retention level if you, in addition to mimicking them, imagine pictures over their heads. Imagine you are watching a live comic strip and a little cloud filled with pictures is floating above the person's head. The pictures above their head should obviously relate to what is being said. It helps reinforce what is being said, while you're still listening and mimicking.

Using the picture exercise will additionally reinforce the words of the speaker and increase your retention. This is another exercise in using your imagination.

How can you get interested in a boring speaker?

Yes! You finally have it—use your imagination! You can have the speaker change appearance. If the speaker is talking about Mozart, have the speaker become Mozart. If the teacher is dissecting a frog, have the teacher become a frog, or a hula dancer, or a policeman, or a sky diver—it doesn't matter; *you* decide. Your imagination is limitless! *You* can make it exciting! When you become involved and interested, you will retain more information and make even the most boring teachers fun (think about it, you know who they are).

Another way to stretch your imagination and help you concentrate, is for *you* to become someone different. This will make the lecture, or speech, or sermon more interesting. One of my trainers told me about a teacher who had all the kids in science class dress up in white coats. He had them "pretend" they actually were scientists, and that they were there to discover something great. The interest level of all those students was amazing. The subject matter stayed the same. Their imagination just changed their association base; they created their own reality. Which way do you think is more fun?

> "I'll tell them Kimberly! You see, there are some awesome teachers out there, and I'm sure you either are one or you have some teaching you. Just give them a chance. A good teacher is a true gift. It took me a while to learn this and appreciate them. If they were boring, I just used my imagination to make them do all sorts of bizarre things, some of which Kimberly won't let me share. Good luck!"

Can you think of any other way you can expand this? This is a gift to yourself, to liven up even the dullest of speakers, retain the information, and best of all have fun in the process. If it's difficult for you to imagine different things at first, be patient with yourself, but *don't ever give up!* Keep trying. Learning to stretch your imagination is like learning anything—to be really good at it you need to practice. Before reading on, I want you to practice this one, because if you don't reinforce it now, it may be harder to inspire you later. (I doubt it though, because you are on your way to becoming an **EmpowerMind** expert!) Hey, practice it at the dinner table tonight. It is really fun to do with the family. I'm sure you'll come up with some really wild stuff. Good luck!

Triggers

Hey, I said don't read on until you try practicing the last section. I mean it. If you read too much without practicing, it may be overwhelming. The most important thing throughout this process is that you have fun!

It is time to test out "triggers." What are they, are they dangerous, and do you have to have a license to carry one? Noooooo. It's not that kind of trigger. *These* triggers can bring you happiness: A's on tests, less study time, laughter and fun.

Triggers are unique to each individual, just like imaginations are unique to each individual. Triggers are simply words or things that remind you of something else. You can create any triggers you choose. There are no rules. You make them up as you go along. Thoroughly confused yet? Oh, good, then it's time for an example.

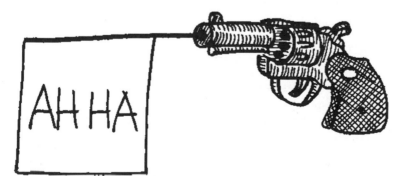

Let's look at the assignment of learning the states. Let's say one teacher wants you to memorize them in alphabetical order. You can do as follows:

Alabama. What does it remind you of, what trigger will help you remember this state? This process is similar to learning the twenty objects; you are just creating another association base. I'm going to help you with the first few states, then you can practice a few more, just to prove to yourself that you can do it. Yes, you too, can be trigger happy in the safety of your own home.

Now, you need to look at the big picture of how to learn these. There are always options. This is trigger example number one.

Alabama: Reminds me of "Album"
Alaska: Reminds me of "Eskimos"
Arizona: Reminds me of "Cactus"
Arkansas: Reminds me of "Ark"
California: Reminds me of "Gold"
Colorado: Reminds me of John "Denver"
Connecticut: Reminds me of "Connect a Cut"

Now, *mentally imagine:*

1. An album on a table
2. Two Eskimos kissing on top of the album
3. A cactus emerging between the Eskimos' lips
4. Noah's Ark balancing on top of the cactus
5. Gold filling up the ark
6. The gold is melting and dripping on John Denver's face
7. John Denver's face is getting all cut up; therefore, he needs to "connect a cut"

Did you make pictures in your mind? You need to *see* it in your mind. Now, repeat them. (It will be much easier when you eventually create your own, by using your own imagination.)

1. _____

2. _____

3. _____

4. _____

5. _____

6. _____

7. _____

Now, you try using your imagination. Remember, the trigger can be anything that reminds you of the state. It doesn't necessarily have to sound like the state.

Delaware: _____

Florida: _____

Georgia: _____

Hawaii: _____

Idaho: _____

Illinois: _____

Indiana: _____

Iowa: _____

Kansas: _____

Kentucky: _____

Now, put these pictures together. Remember, attach two at a time, then drop the state in front and add the next state to the picture. Look back on my example of the first seven states if you need help.

1. _____

2. _____

3. _____

4. _____

5. _____

6. _____

7. _____

8. _____

9. _____

10. _____

Well, how did you do? Test yourself and see. I'll bet you did a lot better than if you hadn't had the triggers. Triggers are your cheat sheet; they help you just like a cheat sheet would. Except, as I said earlier, triggers are legal!

Let's try another kind of trigger. Did you also notice that there are four states that begin with an "A," there are three that begin with a "C," one with a "D," and one with a "F?" Maybe it's easier for you to remember the states by using triggers that represent the first letter of every state.

Let's see how this would look.

4-Apples, three Cats, one Dog and a Fire truck (Connect these pictures.)

Alabama	Alaska	Arizona
Arkansas	California	Colorado
Connecticut	Delaware	Florida

When you connect the pictures in a way you can relate to them, you will remember them. (Or you may just remember how many letters of each state there are by simply looking at the letters. If that is the case, you would save yourself the step of making pictures.)

Then, when you are trying to recall the states, you can think of the pictures to trigger the first letter of each state. By recalling the first letter of each state, you can figure out alphabetically which order they are in. This method won't give you the trigger for each state, like the picturing method did. However, this method will give you the triggers for the letters of the states and how many states start with each letter.

There are many ways to use triggers when trying to memorize…anything. You may think of a way that I haven't. I hope so!

Let's stick with the states a minute here. Let's say you have to know where they all are on the map. You can use a variation on this trigger game to remember where they go.

I think the map on the next page will explain itself.

Now, do you see what you can do here? You can begin with any state and use triggers however you choose. For instance, starting with California and going to the right, the first letter of the first seven states on the bottom spell the words "CAN'T LAG." (California, Arizona, New Mexico, Texas, Louisiana, Alabama, Georgia.) Whoops, I *"missed"* one, between the "L" and the "A." Which one do you think that is? It's Mississippi, of course.

You would have to remember that Florida is at the bottom, but I'm assuming you know where Disney World is on the map. If you are familiar with the states' names and their general locations, this would probably work as a start for you.

Now, let's go the other way (up and over to the left) with our picture method. We have an ore (Oregon) stuck in a washing machine (Washington). When you look in the washing machine you see potatoes (Idaho). Joe Montana is wearing a

coat in the north because it is cold (North Dakota). The coat had a soda spilled all over it (Minnesota).

Try to fill in the rest with your own triggers.

Do you understand what I am doing here? I hope so, because this is a key to testing bliss. You can figure out other ways to remember the states in the middle. You hold the key, it's you who can pull, push, characterize, and exaggerate the trigger. Once you learn how this works for you; it is limitless.

Senses

You have already learned that people learn differently, according to their association bases. Let's take this a step further. People also learn differently based on how they receive information. Some people are: visual learners, auditory learners, kinesthetic learners, tactile learners, learners by smell and taste and some people learn from their intuition. So, what does this mean in English? It means we all learn from specific senses. Some learn by: getting physically involved, touching, smelling or tasting, getting in touch with how they are feeling, seeing or hearing information. Most people learn from a combination of senses. In fact, the more senses you can use together, to learn, the greater success you have in learning.

Which sense(s) do you learn from? Fill out the chart below. The left side has "things that come naturally." It means, what are things that are easy and fun for you to do in your life? Is it watching movies, talking, listening, playing sports, listening to music, sewing, drawing etc.? Just simply write these things in the left column. Do it now!

Talents or Activities That Come Naturally	*Senses Used*
_____	_____
_____	_____
_____	_____
_____	_____
_____	_____
_____	_____
_____	_____
_____	_____
_____	_____

I'll bet you didn't even realize how many natural talents you have. Well, now I want you to write in the right column, the senses used the most with the activity you wrote in the left column. So, you might write "cooking" in the left column and "tasting and smelling" across from it in the right column. Or you might write "watching movies" in the left column and "seeing/visual" in the right column. You may write a sport in the left column and "seeing/visual" and "physically getting involved/tactile or kinesthetic" in the right column. OK, do it now before reading further.

Look now and see which senses you use the most. You might use a combination. Using a combination of your senses is good, too, because you can receive information in several different ways.

If all your answers seem to be visual, that's OK, too. It just means that when you are learning something, you need to make it a picture or some type of visual image in order to learn it easily. If you learn by listening (auditory), you can learn effectively by listening to speakers or tapes. If you are a tactile or kinesthetic learner (you learn by touching or getting involved physically), then you should feel what it is you are learning, or physically get involved in the subject matter. This may include role-playing, acting it out, or touching parts of your body while you learn the subject matter.

Would you like some more examples on how to learn by touching or physically getting involved? Well, either way, you're getting some. Here are a few of my favorites. At Bayside MLK School in Sausalito, the students had to learn what the words "product," "quotient," "sum" and "difference" meant. So, I asked them to become a product in their imaginations (a stereo, box of tissue, video game...whatever they wanted). My favorite product was George's. He chose to become "Brand X." I liked that one the most because "X" is what the word "product" means—to multiply; and the symbol for multiplication is, of course, an X. I had each student draw an X across his/her body to remember their product had an X drawn across it.

To remember "difference," I brought two students up to the front of the class. They had many "differences." One was tall and light, the other was short and dark. I had them stand together, so they could see and experience the "differences" between each other. Then, I physically took one away. It was easy for them to remember that "difference" meant "subtract." Now, you try and figure one out for "quotient" and "divide." How can you physically get involved to remember them. It can really be fun to stretch your imagination this way. Learning can become so easy, if this is how you learn.

If you are a person who learns by getting involved, you may also memorize best by putting the words to music and dancing. You may even sing the words.

(When I do this, I make sure the room I'm singing in has thick walls. You don't have to be a good singer for it to work.) Maybe, as you see the pictures in your mind, you could act out those pictures with your hands or with some type of motion. Try this next time you have to learn something. Translate it into the sense you learn from best. Make a rap song out of a speech, or dance to the song, or put historical facts into a poem, or dress up like a character you are learning about. Get involved with your senses, with the senses that make learning easy for you! Use your awesome imagination! Good luck. I'm sure you will be excited with your results and your interest in the subject.

Summary

By simply using the three techniques in this chapter: *Triggers, Focusing* and *Senses*, you will see an amazing change in your attitude about learning. These techniques will help you make teachers, subjects, and learning in general, a lot more fun. Triggers are like having cheat-sheets in class; and only you can create them for yourself, based on your own imagination. Only you can bring the fun back into learning.

Questions

1. One way to concentrate is to:
    A. Talk along with the speaker.
    B. Make pictures in your mind of what the speaker is saying.
    C. Ask the person next to you if s/he is hearing the same thing you are hearing.
    D. Don't do anything but study.

2. We think _____ as fast as we talk.
   A. Twice
   B. Almost twenty times
   C. Almost ten times
   D. Four times

3. What does mimicking mean?_____

   _____

4. Triggers are (choose the best answer):
   A. Letters
   B. Numbers
   C. Cheat-sheets
   D. Anything that reminds you of something
   E. None of the above

5. True or False? You can use triggers for all learning. _____

6. Triggers also help us:
   A. Retain information longer.
   B. Have fun while learning
   C. Make learning easy
   D. All of the above

7. Why do we remember things better when we use triggers? _____

   _____

   _____

8. Triggers are almost like taking a mental _____ into class.

9. True or False? The trigger method is the only way for you to remember and retain the names of the states well._____

10. Can people learn from more than one sense at a time? _____

11. There are:
    A. Six senses we learn from
    B. Five senses we learn from
    C. Only really three senses that pertain to learning
    D. None of the above

12. You make a class or speaker more fun. You can imagine yourself or the teacher becoming_____ .

"I Can"

Figure it out for yourself, my lad,
You've all that the greatest of men have had:
Two arms, two hands, two legs, two eyes,
And a brain to use if you would be wise.
With this equipment, they all began.
Do start from the top and say, "I can."

Look them over, the wise and the great;
They take their food from a common plate,
And similar knives and forks they use,
With similar laces, they tie their shoes.
The world considers them brave and smart,
But you've all they had when they made their start.

You can triumph and come to skill,
You can be great if you only will.
You're well equipped for what fight you choose;
You have arms legs and a brain to use,
And the man who has risen, great deeds to do,
Began his life with no more than you.

You are the handicap you must face;
You are the one who must choose his place.
You must say what you want to do,
How much to study, the truth to know;
God has equipped you for life, but He
Let's YOU decide what you want to be.

Courage must come from the soul within,
The man must furnish the will to win.
So figure it out for yourself, my lad;
You were born with all that the great have had;
With your equipment, they all began.
Get a hold of yourself and say: "I CAN!"

— *George Washington Carver*

Chapter Four

Discover Your Inner Genius

Overview

This chapter is about understanding and experiencing the power and capability of your brain. We're going to touch on your conscious mind, and deeply explore the realm of your subconscious mind. If you have questions you want to answer, or if you have a problem you need to solve, this chapter will help you. You are going to discover things you never knew existed. You will find out why you are the way you are. This is an incredibly powerful chapter. Are you ready to explore the depths of your mind? Ahh, just as I thought...read on!

Questions

1. True or False. Your subconscious and conscious mind are really the same; they just use different words.

2. Your subconscious mind cannot tell the difference between _____ and _____ . That is why when you put a message in it, the same message comes out.

3. Our filter in our conscious mind is:
   A. Our parents
   B. Our teachers
   C. Our peers
   D. A thing that makes us focus only on what we are interested in.

4. The conscious mind:
   A. Records and stores everything
   B. Creates Self-esteem
   C. Solves Problems

D. All of the above

E. None of the above

5. The subconscious mind can:

    A. Help you create whatever you want for yourself in your life.

    B. Make you react inappropriately to situations.

    C. Build up anger

    D. All of the above

6. Once we have lost our memory:

    A. It is gone forever

    B. It is hidden until a trigger brings it back

    C. It's never really gone unless we've had brain damage

    D. Both B and C

    E. None of the above

Let's start out simply. What is your conscious mind? Do you even know? Your conscious mind is your awareness of your existence, thoughts, and surroundings. Your conscious mind only rules about 10% or less of your whole mind. If it only rules 10% of your mind, let's find out what it does.

Are you conscious now? Let's see if you are. Without, and I *repeat*, *without* looking away from this book or in any other direction, I want you to tell me the color of the walls, type and color of the floor, the pictures on the walls and basically *all* the details of where you are. If you're outside, do the same thing. Shut your eyes now and think about it.

Did you get the details of at least half of the surroundings right? If you didn't, it's OK. Most people are not real conscious. If you do what this chapter says you will be conscious most of the time. If you didn't do too well on this assignment, it's most likely due to your lack of interest in the details of your surroundings. You see, your mind likes to focus on things that it is interested in, *not* on details it couldn't care less about. So, don't be hard on yourself if you can't remember the color of your socks right now. Can you? See, it isn't life threatening if you forget the color of your socks—unless you are dressing a model to perform in public or you are in the design business.

I just *love* using this assignment in my classes. I'll have people shut their eyes and tell me the colors of the door, ceiling, rug, and walls. I'll ask them about things on the walls and on the furniture. It has been amazing! Most people get them *all* wrong! It is *very* humbling. If you don't believe that people could really be this "unaware" of the details of their surroundings, then go out and do a test.

Practice on your friends the next time you see them. If you're at a restaurant, ask them to close their eyes. Then, ask them detailed questions about the surroundings. I think you will be amazed. If you have an interior designer among the group s/he will probably do better than the rest of the group (unless s/he's nervous or upset for some reason). Why will s/he do so well? You tell me. It's because s/he's interested in it!

What else do you know about the conscious mind? Well, it does some things automatically. What does it do automatically? Good question! Think of yourself outside on a beautiful day. All of a sudden, you see some dark clouds and a wind picks up. Instantly, it begins to hail (they are big buggers, too) on your head. Your conscious mind goes through an automatic process here. It perceives the environment, associates it (to past experience, of course), evaluates it, then makes a decision about what to do. This all happens within seconds, often in even less time. You can choose to take cover, put up an umbrella, stand on your head, or be just plain macho and take it like a person who...loves pain? Whatever you decide isn't important here; explaining the natural process of your conscious mind is what's important.

Another asset (and problem) the conscious mind has is called a "reticular activating system."

"Woooo! That's a mouth full! Keep it simple Kimberly, so the readers (that's you adults, too) can understand it. Or they'll get to play detective, like you suggested I do, and keep a dictionary next to them when they read this book. That's fine for other books, but yours is different. You always told me 'keep it simple!' "

Hacker, you're right again! A reticular activating system is really a filter system. It can be both an asset and a problem. Our conscious mind filters things all the time based on what we are interested in.

Have you ever asked your mom whether there's some type of food in your house, because *you* haven't seen it? You are sure it's not there, but your mom comes up and points it out to you.

Has someone ever told you that a building is right next to a place you have passed, for years, and you don't believe him or her? But lo and behold, it *is* there.

Have you ever listened to a lecture, movie, pastor or person, with friends—and they seemed to hear a different message than you did?

Think of some other times you saw something one way, when other people saw it another. Maybe you didn't see it at all. This does *not* mean that you're stupid! It just means that you have a different filter system and your interests are different.

These filter systems are good and bad. Sometimes they protect you, because if you take in too much information, it will be overwhelming. Many highly intuitive people can take in a great deal of information all at the same time. They can use all their senses and they're super conscious at the same time.

Do you remember the story in the newspapers about a woman whose daughter triggered a memory for her? She went into hypnosis and remembered that, when she was a child, her father killed her best friend. She hadn't remembered it because her filter system was protecting her. The tragedy was always in her brain, but her conscious mind wasn't ready to accept and deal with it. Her conscious mind filtered information from her subconscious mind.

Many times we consciously block out painful events to protect ourselves. Some events are too horrible to remember. We cannot bring in all the information we experience consciously, because it would be on overload and we'd probably need some professional counseling. Imagine if you noticed every single detail: the smells of people, the past energy in the room, the sounds that are still in the walls, etc. It would blow your mind, and you might end up in a hospital for the mentally ill. The filters are a good thing. They filter out stuff we don't need.

Is it ever bad that you have these filters? What do you think? Sometimes, wouldn't it be nice to know what people are thinking, or what the teacher thinks should be on the tests, or every detail of a mystery? Sometimes, it would. You will be able to control this filter system a little better once you learn more about how the subconscious connects it all together. You will learn how the subconscious works as you keep reading this book.

SUBCONSCIOUS

CREATIVITY

AUTOMATIC FUNCTIONS

RECORDS AND STORES

ASSOCIATIONS/FILTERS

SOLVES PROBLEMS

SELF-ESTEEM

Subconscious

We are going to move into the exciting exploration of the subconscious. What is the subconscious, anyway? Do you *really* know? It is the other 90+ percent of your brain that guides, defines and supports you through life. Remember, the conscious mind directs less than 10 percent of the mind; the subconscious directs the rest. It is the complete mental process of which an individual is not aware. What the heck does that mean? Well, it's kind of like a space ship. On a space ship, you might see a bubble at the top in which there are a pilot and some crew members. The pilot is the controller of the ship, but it's really the machinery, technology, and extra crew below that make the ship operate so successfully. Your subconscious is simply the bottom of the space ship.

One of the first characteristics I want you to know about your subconscious mind is, it is the place where you have all your *"creativity."* Your creativity emerges from your subconscious. This is why some days you seem to be more creative than others; it simply emerges from your subconscious. Wouldn't it be nice if you could control this and be creative when you choose to be creative? Naturally, it cannot be controlled. That is why some days you are more effective, quick-witted, have better solutions, are more artistic, etc., than others. Creativity simply comes at certain times versus other times. When you learn to get into a relaxed state of mind—the alpha state—you can actually control when you become creative. You will learn about this in the Alpha Bliss chapter. For now, all you need to know is that creativity emerges from the subconscious mind.

The subconscious mind also takes care of all your *"automatic functions."* What do you think automatic functions are? What automatic functions does your body have that you don't consciously think about? How about: blinking, breathing, blood flowing, hair and nails growing? These are automatic functions.

"Kimberly, isn't it true that you don't 'consciously' make them happen, they just naturally happen. I mean, isn't that what our subconscious is all about?"

You've got it Hacker!

Now, shut your eyes and think of the same alien you thought about in Chapter One. Come on....

OK now; whatever the features of your alien were, they were drawn upon from your subconscious. I'm assuming you haven't actually seen an alien (*yet*) but rather you are pulling up a picture from your subconscious that represents what you have seen, that looks like an alien from your past (i.e., books, comics, television, movies, etc.).

Let's see what little information people have learned about the subconscious so far. Your subconscious **"*records and stores*"** everything you have *ever* seen. Yes, even the color of the shoe laces you wore when you were a baby. Yes, *even* the hospital where you were born. It seems amazing that you can remember every word that has been said to you and every detail of every detail that you have seen. Do I sound nuts? Well, that's beside the point. I am giving you accurate information.

I'll bet you are asking, if this is true, then why *can't* I remember all of those things in my life? The answer is that you can. You don't lose memory, just triggers to the memory (unless you have had brain damage). Have you ever walked down a street or walked into a house and smelled a smell that reminded you of your childhood? You actually had forgotten the memory until you smelled the smell? That is proof right there. It's in your brain, it's just buried. Some professionals believe hypnosis is very effective, and they use it to help their clients remember everything. I will get back to this in a minute. But first, I think I may be losing you, so I'll give you some more facts.

As you learn more and more about the subconscious mind, the less amazing it will really seem. Remember, our brains are like computers, but they are hundreds of times more effective, *and* we only use less than ten percent of them. If this is true, wouldn't it make sense that if we created a camera lens, we could record at least the pictures, in our heads? Think about it. Our eyes are awesome lenses. They can see for miles. They can see details and remember them. They can also record these details better than a little man-made camera. It just takes us, like pictures, time to develop them.

When we are taken out of our conscious mind and put back into our subconscious mind where all the developing has already taken place, we can remember better. The pictures are there, we just need to be in our alpha state to see them again. (We'll talk about the alpha state later.) This is what many of the psychology experts think hypnosis achieves for their clients.

Many students in my courses ask me, "If all of this is possible, then why can't I do it when I'm relaxed and in my alpha state?" The reason is, because like everything, mastering a subject takes a lot of practice. To be able to access your subconscious mind for *any* information takes years of training and practice. Most people aren't committed to it enough to spend the time on it. Just imagine, if our brains are *this* powerful, what would happen if you learned to use even one percent more of yours? I hope you answered, "A lot!"

You see, because the subconscious mind takes in so much, you need to be careful about what you expose yourself to on a daily basis. Yes, those of you who watch an excessive amount of TV will be negatively affected. Those of you who are exposed to negative people, over a long period of time, will be damaged. Those of you from abusive homes will be damaged in some way. This doesn't mean you can't reverse it. Your subconscious mind remembers everything, so if you listen to it, intuitively, you can learn from it. Hang in there, you will learn how to reverse it as you continue reading.

I have also had students ask me, "If we have so many brain cells, what matters if a few of them are killed off by alcohol and drugs?" The problem is that we cannot selectively choose which brain cells we are going to kill. You may be carrying the brain cell that has the memory of drawing stored in it, or maybe the memory of how to concentrate in sports, or maybe the memory of how much *your life has to offer* this world. No, one glass of wine with dinner will not damage you for life, but drugs in *any* form will damage your brain. If you want the most from your brain's potential, **do not do drugs!** You'll lose a few percentage points of total brain usage by using drugs. I certainly will not preach (that *never* does much good, anyway). You are an intelligent young adult. All I want you to know is that there are alternatives to pain. You do *not* have to do drugs to numb yourself. What I would

like to do is present some facts to you, and explain *why* you may feel the way you do about the choices you have made. You can decide what makes sense and, I hope, you will make some healthy choices in the future. It's *never* too late! I believe you will choose wisely. In fact, I'll bet another pizza on it!

Now you know that the brain records and stores all information and it can be reached through hypnosis. Hundreds of studies have been done to prove this. Scientists and doctors have exposed people to situations, then asked them what they saw. The people usually have something very limited to say in response. But when hypnotized, they remember *everything* about their experience.

Here's an example. Did you see the movie, *Rainman*? In this movie, Dustin Hoffman was an autistic savant. Autistic means "extreme withdrawal into fantasy." Savant means "a person of profound or extensive learning." This character could remember numbers like a computer. He had the capability to remember sequences and numbers as well as any computer. Unfortunately, that was about the only area in which he could excel. His "reticular activating system" was *very* limited. It was as though he were programmed. People like this exist in the world. They have the capability to recall information like computers. You have this capability too, but your reticular activating system is too interested in "other" things to get all caught up in just numbers.

Knowing your brain has this capability helps you understand why hypnosis works so well with people who are looking at deep-seated problems from their childhood. You know that our brains record *everything*. Knowing this helps people remember, in detail, what happened, so they can work on resolving it. Hypnosis is useful, but you can learn to tap into your subconscious on your own. How? You will find out in the next chapter of the book.

What other amazing things is your subconscious capable of achieving? You know that it can do two things already. It _____ and _____ information.

Two more features the subconscious mind has are creating *"associations and filters."* The associations and filters I am referring to are the ones which originated in your brain at the beginning. It is true that your subconscious mind records everything and creates associations and filters based on your past experiences. These original associations and filters ultimately create conscious filters.

It is time for you to use your imagination again. When you were much younger, a lot of your friends were mean to you, didn't follow up with plans, and even stood you up a lot. It happened most of the time, but you have put it out of your conscious mind. You are much older now. You have a date scheduled with someone on whom you have a mad crush. It is a first date and you are meeting somewhere. This person is twenty minutes late (which isn't really that big of a deal). You are not just getting worried, but a surge of anger is building up inside you. The date finally comes and you are overly angry at the person for being late. It's like you don't even want to listen to excuses, because you feel as if they will be lies anyway. Your reaction may have nothing to do with what is happening. You may not even have a clue as to *why* you feel this way. It's all association and filters, created in the past, that are emerging from your subconscious. There are memories lodged there that you may not even be aware you're experiencing.

Let's say someone walks into a room with a stick held up over his/her head, and you get all nervous and panicky. It could be because it is something that is being triggered from your subconscious. Maybe you were beaten with a stick as a child, and your dad held it over his head. It may be so painful, that you don't "consciously" know, but subconsciously you do and your body reacts.

As in all relationships and incidences, there seems to be three realities: your version, the other person's version and — "the truth."

> **"THUS, THE PRIMARY
> CHARACTERISTIC
> OF A TRUE LEADER
> IS THE SAME AS THAT OF
> A PHILOSOPHER;
> TO BE PASSIONATELY IN LOVE
> WITH THE TRUTH."**
>
> *Robert Rabbin*

Do people ever think you overreact to things? Or do you get angry a lot? If you do overreact to some situations, those situations probably triggered something that happened to you in your past—that you cannot consciously remember. Just think about it. Your reaction is most likely based on memories that are lodged in your subconscious mind. Most of our reactions are based on information that is stored in our subconscious. This is where our original associations and filters are formed.

The subconscious also *"solves problems"* for us. This is a really neat thing to learn. When you get into your alpha state (I'll bet you're getting excited about finding out what that is) you can program your mind to give you an answer. All your brain cells just send messages to each other, check all your past experiences and give you an answer. I'm simplifying it, but you will know exactly what I'm talking about after these examples—and after you have an actual experience with it by listening to the tape. The tape can be ordered by filling out and sending in the form in the back of this book.

Have you ever had a person's or an actor's name on the tip of your tongue, but it just didn't come out? You can push and force it all you want, but you just cannot come up with it? Then, you go about doing your business, and you're

walking down the hall, washing the dishes, or just watching cars go by and, *presto*, magically the name appears out of nowhere! It doesn't really appear out of nowhere—your subconscious mind has been working on it from the moment you asked it for the information. Have you ever left a test and as soon as you were out of the room remembered the answer you couldn't figure out? The reason this happens is that when you are uptight, your mind cannot access information from your subconscious. It automatically shuts off, but when you relax, it simply works for you and gives you the answer.

Let's put this theory to practice. I want you to write a question to a person. This person is the wisest person in the world. I want you to ask this person for an answer to a problem in your life, or something personal that you would like an answer to. Write it now, as though you were actually going to send it to this wise person.

Dear Wise Person:

_____

_____

_____

_____

_____

_____

_____

You'll see later how this works, so hang in there.

The last thing I will mention that the subconscious does (*that I know of*), is it creates our "*self-esteem.*" It programs who we are in our lives. It tells us if we are good or bad, smart or dumb, attractive or unattractive, etc. This is all programming that we learn *very* early in our lives. It varies with each person, because it is *all* based on our past experience.

When you are born, you are like an empty computer with no programming. Well, you do have a few basics. You want to be loved, nurtured and supported. That's it! Then, you get some programming from the outside that tells you who you are. Who do you think does this? Who puts in all sorts of information? Who did you think was God when you were a child? Who did you look up to as a small child? *Who programmed you*? Yes, it was your...parents. They put in good stuff and bad stuff. Parents aren't perfect because humans aren't perfect; that is why

you may have received some bad programming.

I'm going to ask you to use your imagination again. I want you to read these next stories and think about which one or combination of the two represents your life.

"This goes for all you adults, too."

There is a little girl named Kathy. She is in kindergarten and has just drawn a beautiful picture in school. She is very excited about it and can't wait to show her teacher, Ms. Thompson. She finally gets a chance to show Ms. Thompson the picture. She's all smiles, because she is very proud. Ms. Thompson looks at the picture and is elated! She says, "Kathy, this is *so* original. You drew an extra animal that wasn't there before. You made purple trees and beautiful orange streams. You are so creative! After you show your parents, I want to hang this on the board so other kids can learn from you." Kathy is so happy, she can hardly stand her excitement.

She runs home and pulls the picture out, with a huge smile on her face. Her mom looks at it and says, "You did it again! You created another masterpiece. I especially love how you zoomed out of the lines over here, and had the stream run right into the tree." She hugs her and they start laughing together. Dad overhears this and says, "Hey, what am I missing here?" Mom says, "Our Kathy did it again! She is a genius!" She shows him the picture. Dad puts on his glasses and looks closely. He falls over backwards and onto the floor. "The colors," he exclaims. "They are so bright and beautiful; they just knocked me over." They all start

laughing and rolling around on the floor.

Now, how do you think Kathy feels when she gets another drawing project in kindergarten? Do you think she is excited? She not only gets excited, but she helps the other kids be more creative with their pictures. She is always excited to try a new way to do something. Kathy knows that she can do anything, and that she doesn't always have to stay in the lines, follow all the rules. To be successful; in fact, when she steps a bit out of the lines, she produces more. She becomes confident and does things in a way no one has ever done. She now owns her own company helping other people learn to be creative through art expression. She loves life!

Now, there is Kathy number two. She is in kindergarten and has just drawn a beautiful picture. She is very excited about it and can't wait to show her teacher, Ms. Thompson. She finally gets a chance to show Ms. Thompson the picture. She's all smiles, because she is very proud. Ms. Thompson looks at the picture and is dismayed. She says, "Kathy, don't you know that trees aren't purple, and streams aren't orange? Don't you know that you can't draw outside the lines?" Maybe you will do better next time when you follow the rules."

Kathy is upset, of course, but she tries to convince herself that her mom will see the beauty in her picture. Dad...well, he left home some time ago, and when he visits, there's always a fight. He's never satisfied. Her mom has only criticized the things she's done in the past, but Kathy is hoping. She goes home and shows

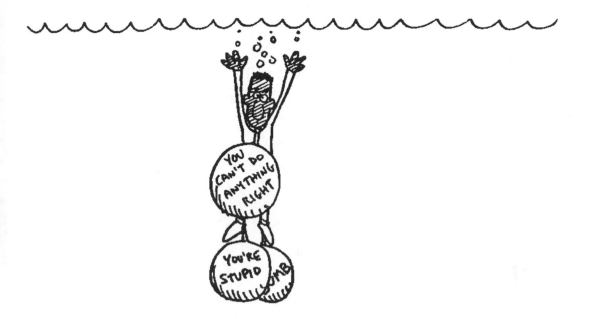

her mom the picture. Her mom is dismayed and frustrated. She starts to yell. "Kathy, don't you know how to do anything right? Skies are blue, not rainbow colored, trees are green and brown *not* purple. Can't you stay in the lines?!"

There is a knock at the door and her dad comes in. He overheard the tail-end of the yelling. He asks, "What's all this yelling about?"

"Oh, Kathy screwed up again," her mom answers. Kathy is really scared now; she just can't believe it. They did it again!

Dad says, "Oh, I think you're probably too hard on her, let me see what she did wrong?" Mom shows him the picture. *He* just laughs at it and says "It's all screwed up, but who cares? I can't believe you ever thought she'd do better than this. We've both seen what she's done in the past. Besides, school doesn't matter; she'll never even finish high school. I didn't—and what does it matter anyway?"

Kathy is devastated.

How do you think she feels when she gets another drawing project in kindergarten? Do you think she is excited? She not only is scared to draw, but she's scared about trying. She never steps out of the lines. She loses her creativity. She was a creative genius, but now, she just stays in the lines and follows the rules. She becomes boring and isn't real excited about trying new things anymore. In fact, school becomes so boring she figures, "Why even try anymore?" She drops out of high school. Does any of this sound familiar?

Stop and think! Which Kathy was more capable? Was it Kathy number one or Kathy number two? If you answered that they both had the same capability, you are right. What was the difference? It was programming—parental programming. Which one was more like you and your upbringing, or was there a little bit of both? Do you see how strongly your parents influence you about *who you are*? Most parents do the best they can. They probably had similar upbringings to the one you have. They are human. They can give you a lot of garbage, or you can simply filter situations improperly. It is up to *you* to change your negative programming.

> "Kimberly, you are totally right on! I have had major negative programming. I've been given the ultimate garbage from my mom and dad."

So, Hacker, do you have anything to say to your peers?

> "Hang in there, man. Believe in yourself. 'Cuz in the end it's totally up to you."

You said it Hacker! Later in this chapter, and in Chapter Nine, you will learn where to get support that will help you believe in yourself. Until then...

Something *very* important to know in this chapter is that your subconscious cannot tell the difference between imagination and reality. I repeat, your subconscious cannot tell the difference between imagination and reality. Can I prove this? Well, of course I can! Have you ever had a dream where you were falling? Do you remember jerking awake because your whole body really felt like you were falling?

Your subconscious CANNOT tell the difference between imagination and reality.

Have you ever had someone remind you of someone else, and you either had a positive or negative reaction to the person that you couldn't explain?

Imagine that you are in a 120 degree desert. You haven't had a drink of water in days and it feels like cotton balls are filling your mouth. You're getting hotter and hotter by the second. The cotton balls are completely filling your mouth. (Geez, I'm having a reaction just writing it!) Use your imagination, shut your eyes and imagine that happening to you.

Well, have I convinced you yet? I have one more example you may try, in the safety of your home. Have a friend stand up and put his/her arm out. Have the friend shut his/her eyes and imagine the arm becoming a steel rod. Really play it up and have the friend get into it. (Repeat how strong this powerful steel rod is several times.) Then try to push the arm down. See how much resistance you get. Now, try it again, but this time, while the arm is still stretched out, say this twice,

"Your arm feels as light as a feather; in fact, it almost is rubbery. It is weak and getting weaker. You can hardly hold it up. It's almost got a force pulling it down." Now, try and pull it down. Your friend will have little to *no* resistance. You try it! I can guarantee that one of these examples will prove to you that the subconscious mind believes what we put into it.

It's up to you to start re-programming your mind. Sometimes you may have such a "*set way*" of acting and reacting, that when you get new information, it's like putting a square peg in a round hole—it just doesn't fit or make sense. So, it may take some time; but after a while it will become familiar. This takes practice. *Begin* with one step at a time. See yourself accomplishing things. See yourself, in your mind, being confident on a date or at a party. Keep telling yourself how wonderful you really are. Tell yourself that you will get A's on tests and that you will study in half the time it used to take you. Guess what? It will work, because your mind doesn't know the difference. Remember, your subconscious mind

cannot tell the difference between imagination and reality.

What do you think happens when, for years, you have been saying, "I hate math. I can't remember names. I can't speak in front of groups," etc.? I'll tell you what happens. Your little brain cells turn on you. When you walk into math class, and it's time to learn, your little subconscious brain cells say, "WOOOOOOOOOOOOOOOOO, 'MATH' you have got to be kidding! *We* don't *do* math!" They mock you and shut down all learning capability. What you feed in is what you get out. So, start changing your programming. Start *loving* these things you used to hate. Start visualizing success in situations instead of failure. Remember, the subconscious mind cannot tell the difference between _____ and _____.

Our program starts with our parents and is reinforced with our own mental tapes: "I can't, I'll fail, I'm scared, I'm a loser *or* I can do it! I'll try! I'm not so bad. I'm really proud of myself." This is one thing we have control over. If you don't change your negative programming, you will attract negative things in your life. If you have positive programming, you will attract positive things in your life. Put positive poems on your mirror, and read them daily. Surround yourself with positive people who make you feel good about yourself, not those who will only be your friend if you do drugs and get into trouble. Start loving yourself and your whole programming will improve. Believe in yourself, trust yourself and love yourself. The reason you have trouble with peer pressure is because you don't believe in yourself, trust yourself and love yourself. If you really did, you could say, "*No.*"

This next story is kind of like a Kathy number three story. (You may even have your own Kathy "number four" story. Anything is possible.) I have a young teenage friend who was worried about everything: sports, school, girls, that raging hormone thing, etc. I had a heart-to-heart with him one day. He said it was because of his mother. He said that his mom expected so much of him, he could *never* live up to it all. It was driving him nuts! I knew his mother, and it didn't seem like she put all that much pressure on him, at least not intentionally. I asked him what she said exactly. He said, "Well, she always expects such great things from me, because she said I am destined to be great and accomplish great things."

I said, "Are you sure she doesn't mean you will be great because you are so great the way you are right now?" He wasn't convinced. I asked him if he ever talked to her about it. He hadn't, so he really never knew for sure. You see, we have these inborn filters. That is why a parent can do the same thing to two kids in a family, and they can each take the same situation differently. It affects their life by the way they interpret it, not, I repeat, not by what has *actually* happened.

Another woman I met in a psychotherapy workshop had a father who beat

her all the time. He did some very awful things to her and her sisters. He received an award, in his church no less, as the "Father of the Year." It was not only sick, but do you know how that made this little girl feel when she was a child? She thought she must be an awful, terrible person if the rest of the world thought her dad was such a great father. You *never*, I mean you *never* really know what goes on in other people's families, in other peoples' lives. So watch it when you judge someone too harshly. We all have different filter systems.

This next story is about a student who was eliminated as part of the "in group" in his high school class. He is 16 years old. He is gorgeous, sweet, fun, a good athlete and a 4.0 student. Because he doesn't drink and do drugs, but mostly because he is *nice*, he's *not* popular! I *know* nice doesn't seem to "be in" now, but hey, give each other a break. "Nice" does *not* have to mean boring, or that the person has a mad uncontrollable crush on you. Wake up! Nice may just simply mean "nice." It is part of our subconscious programming to do drugs and be a bit aloof, or just be a cool dude to "fit in." If you grew up in a family that drinks a lot, then guess what? You probably will too, because it seems like reality to you. It is comfortable. If your family is mean or aloof, then that explains the negative filters you may have. Aloof and mean are comfortable.

"This chapter really got to me, man. My total home life is pretty crummy, and I used to smoke a lot of pot and drink to be "cool" and to forget my problems. That's really why school was such a drag. I became so lazy and uninterested. The drugs seemed to help, but they also created more problems. Reach out to other people who seem happy and have their lives together—people who aren't doing drugs. They may even be adults or teachers. People care, man. Just give 'em a chance. It may just surprise you. I did and it changed my life."

Thanks, Hacker. Now what can you do about this negative programming you feed yourself? Sometimes, it helps to have a friend, someone you really respect, make a positive programming tape for you. Have the person say all sorts of wonderful things about you, with examples, over and over again for ten minutes into a tape recorder. Then, play it every morning while you are getting ready for your day—until you believe it is true. If you don't have enough good stuff to put on a tape, then start being nicer to people, give your time and your love away. It's guaranteed to come back to you one hundred times over.

If you could get only one thing out of this chapter, I would like you to know that your negative programming is *not* your fault. You had *no* choice as a child. You just received the information and you processed it like computers do. But *now* you can be responsible, because you *know* that you can change, and that you really still are that beautiful baby who just wants to be encouraged, supported and loved. You are perfect just the way you are. The things you *do* or the *trouble* you may get into isn't perfect, but *you* definitely are!

You have the power to make choices for yourself in your life. You will constantly be given one choice after another. Sometimes you will choose wisely, and sometimes...you will *not*. It's OK that you make some wrong choices. (I'll let you in on a secret...adults make wrong choices *all* the time.) Be gentle with yourself and simply learn from your mistakes. *Most* importantly, it is best to be *happy, not* "perfect." You are the one who holds the key to choices in your life. You can be happy and successful—the choice is yours.

Do something really nice for yourself today. Put down this book, after this chapter, and go do something just for you. I like bubble baths and soft music myself. Maybe it's making your favorite food or calling an old friend—long distance. Just do something really nice for you. *You deserve it!*

Summary

You are born perfect. You just want to be loved, encouraged, and supported, but some negative program gets in your way. You have filters that process your information. These filters are generally a distortion of reality. When you learn why your filters are the way they are, then you can understand and even change them. It is never too late to change your negative programming; it just takes time, patience and *practice*.

Questions

1. True or False? Your subconscious and conscious mind are really the same; they just use different words.

2. Your subconscious mind cannot tell the difference between _____ and _____ . That is why when you put a message in it, the same message comes out.

3. Our filter in our conscious mind is
    A. Our parents
    B. Our teachers
    C. Our peers
    D. A thing that makes us focus only on what we are interested in

4. The conscious mind:
    A. Records and stores everything
    B. Creates Self-esteem
    C. Solves Problems
    D. All of the above
    E. None of the above

5. The subconscious mind can:
    A. Help you create whatever you want for yourself in your life
    B. Make you react inappropriately to situations
    C. Build up anger
    D. All of the above

6. Once we have lost our memory:
    A. It is gone forever
    B. It is hidden until a trigger brings it back
    C. It's never really gone unless we've had brain damage
    D. Both B and C
    E. None of the above

7. It's our conscious mind that really:
    A. Controls us
    B. Makes us sick
    C. Makes us happy
    D. Filters information from our subconscious

8. True or False? Self-esteem is created by the subconscious. _____

9. Hypnosis can be used to help us:
    A. Retrieve information from the subconscious
    B. Make *all* of our dreams come true in an instant
    C. Become evil
    D. Discover people who are mentally ill

10. If we take drugs:
    A. We will kill some brain cells, maybe even important ones.
    B. It doesn't matter, because we have approximately one hundred billion brain cells.
    C. We are losers forever.
    D. We are smart. It's a great way to relieve a little tension.
    E. None of the above

11. Our past experience is lodged in detail in our _____ .

12. Sometimes we react to something inappropriately because:
    A. Of information from our past experience
    B. People just make us mad
    C. Of our parents
    D. We're really *all* kids deep down

13. We begin life like a:
    A. Blank computer
    B. Wise person
    C. Screwed up person who just needs some fixing
    D. As a programmed computer

14. True or False? You have the ability to change any programming, no matter how deep it is. _____

15. Life is good to you when you are_____ .

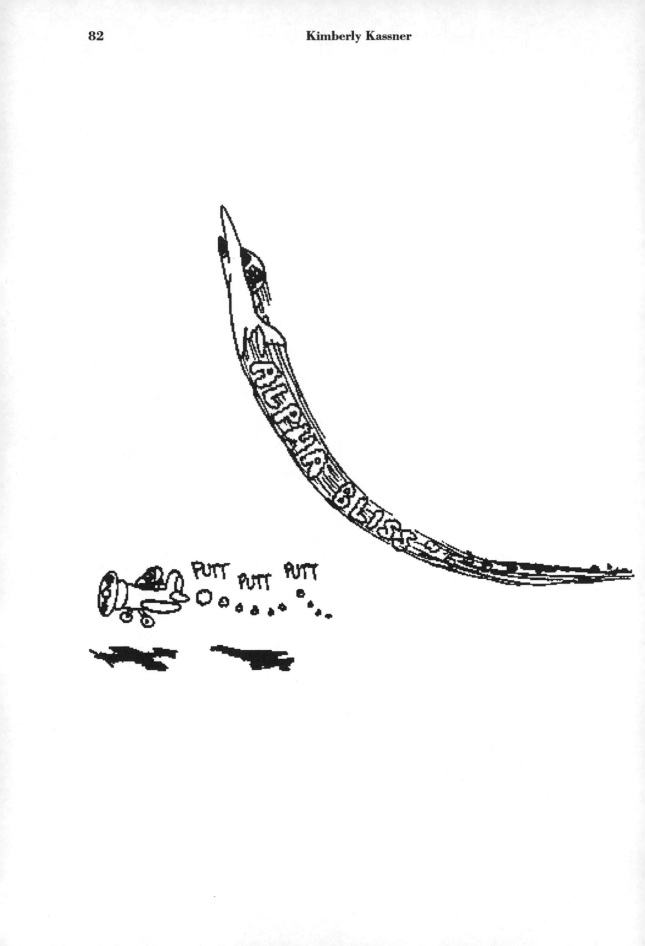

Chapter Five

How To Achieve Peak Performance

Overview

What is alpha bliss? It is the state your mind is in at its optimal performance. It is where athletes break world records; it's being in "the zone." It's where the greatest of motivational speakers are when they speak to groups of 1,000; it is where you are, when you are at your best. It is a state of peacefulness. It is a state of mind where you can tap into your subconscious and retrieve any of the information you have stored there. If you would like to learn how to get to this place and stay there, as much as possible, then read on.

Questions

1. Our brain has brain-wave frequencies. Its ability to communicate is more powerful than man-made inventions with frequencies. Name three of these man-made inventions. _____

   _____

   _____

2. The alpha frequency is between which amount of cycles per second?
   A. 4.5-7.0
   B. 0-18
   C. 7-10
   D. 7-14

3. What brain wave state are people in most of the time?
   A. Alpha
   B. Theta
   C. Sigma Chi
   D. Beta
   E. California

4. What is one way you can get into the alpha state quickly?
    A. Eat sugar
    B. Meditate
    C. Take several deep breaths
    D. Sleep

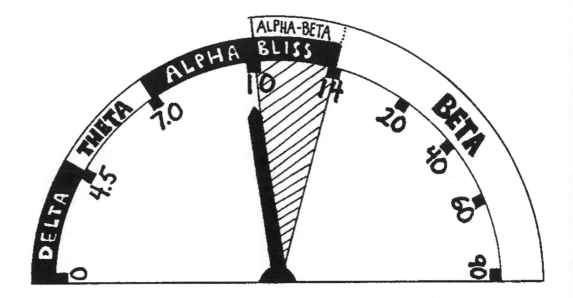

Your brain has brain-wave frequencies just as missiles, microwaves, radios and TV's have frequencies. Your brain waves vibrate at a certain number of cycles per second. If they aren't vibrating at all, guess what?

"Yep! You're dead as a doornail."

You want them to vibrate, but not too slowly. Too slowly is 4.5 cycles per second or less, and is referred to as the Delta State. It is also referred to as the zombie or coma state of mind.

If your brain-wave frequencies are vibrating at the next state, the theta state, they are vibrating at 4.5 to 7.0 cycles per second. This is when you are sleeping, in deep meditation, or just coming out of or are just going into a sleep state.

The state of vibration from seven to fourteen cycles per second is called the *alpha* state. (I refer to it as the alpha bliss.) This is a state of relaxation and peacefulness. This is the place of optimal performance. It occurs when you are just waking up, or meditating to a peaceful relaxed state of consciousness. This is when you are at peace in your mind. You are *not* anxious or filled with worry, you are living in the moment. This is the state of mind where you perform your best. If you could choose any place to be, it should be in the alpha state all the time. This is where you will be the happiest.

The last state, the one you generally live in all the time, is from ten cycles per second on up. This is referred to as the beta state. This is when you are awake and alert. If brain waves vibrate much past fourteen (past the alpha/beta state) then the person tends to become anxious. This is where the general population is most of the time. This is when you are alert and awake, but it is often accompanied by worry, stress, anxiety or fear. Read the next paragraph, then shut your eyes for a minute and do what it says.

Shut your eyes and think of all the people in the world you would like to impress, or just a general group of 500 people. You are going to go out in front of all of them and tell them, in a speech, how they should change their lives to be more successful. Shut your eyes and really feel like you are there.

Well, how are you feeling? Put your hand on your chest. Is your heart beating...faster? OK, if you didn't notice a change, then shut your eyes and think of your next big test. Visualize this test as being a "make or break you" test. Or,

simply shut your eyes and think of something that terrifies you. Maybe it's something that has happened in your past. Now, put your hand on your chest. Is your heart beating...faster? This is the beta state. It is not real great, is it? Then, why is it that we seem to live our lives in this state? It is because we haven't all learned how to stay in our alpha and alpha/beta state. You can change that. You can learn to live in your alpha state more often and tap into your subconscious.

You've heard of "being in the zone" in a sport right? Well, I'd like to show you how to train your mind to be in "the zone" of life as often as possible. I would like you to use the following relaxation script. If you are a teacher, read it to your class, or simply read it slowly and lovingly into an audio tape, then replay the tape to yourself or to your class. This is the suggested method. The tapes are always the most effective when the right person's voice reads the script. Parents and students can also make their own tapes. (Either have someone else read it to you or create your own tape. I suggest you always make a tape.)

"Relaxation audio tapes of both scripts are also available for purchase from EmpowerMind."

Thank you, Hacker! I'm glad you remembered there are tapes from the **EmpowerMind** course (see the order form in the back of the book).

Now let's go! Start with the script entitled "Goals." You or the participants, who will be listening to the script being read, or listening to your homemade tape, or the **EmpowerMind** tape, should sit in a comfortable position and relax before beginning.

Make your mental goal in this relaxation to talk in front of that same group of 500 people, or face whatever fear you would like to overcome. Remember, this time you will see the fear in your mind and see yourself overcome it. It's an amazing feeling. It will really help you overcome your fears. Listen to the script or tape, then write what happened while you visualized overcoming your fear in your alpha state.

Do it before you read on, or it won't work. Remember, if you read it or record it, do it slowly and with appropriate voice inflection.

Goals Script

Welcome to a journey into relaxation through **EmpowerMind**. Think of a goal you would like to achieve in your life. The goal can be associated with school, relationships or work. It can be any goal. Just gently allow the goal to appear in your mind. *(Pause.)*

Now, make sure your arms and legs are uncrossed and that you are in a comfortable position.

Shut your eyes and take a deep breath. *(Pause.)*

This relaxation adventure will naturally match your conscious and subconscious mind, wherever they are.

I will be speaking in first person. When you hear my voice, you will hear it as if it were your own voice talking to yourself.

Now, as I take another deep breath, I imagine a warm soothing white light over my head, relaxing my head. This warm light continues over my forehead, relaxing my forehead, down to my nose relaxing my nose, down to my lips, relaxing my lips, down to my chin, relaxing my chin—until my whole face is bathed in the soothing white light.

The warm soothing light then moves down to my neck, relaxing my neck; it moves down into my shoulders until my shoulders are completely relaxed.

This warm white light moves slowly down from my shoulders into my upper arms, down to my lower arms, then down to my hands and all the way down to my fingertips, until my arms and hands are completely relaxed in this warm soothing white light. *(Pause.)*

The light continues down into my chest. As I take a deep breath and let it out, the light continues to gently glide down my stomach, I feel its warmth. I also notice the light slowly pouring out the back of my neck down my spine, relaxing all the muscles down my spine, one by one, until my back is completely relaxed in the soothing warm white light.

I take another deep breath and notice my whole upper body is completely relaxed in this warm soothing white light. *(Pause.)*

The light continues to move down into my buttocks until they are completely relaxed. It moves down my thighs and down into my calves until my legs are completely relaxed in this soothing white light. Then it moves into my feet, all the way down to my toes until my feet and toes are completely relaxed. Now my whole body is completely relaxed in this warm soothing white light. I slowly move through my body, looking for any tension. If I find tension, I simply concentrate on it and say to myself "Relax." As I take a deep breath, I feel relaxed like I never have before. I am aware of some other sensation. It could be warm, tingly or a floating sensation. This is an indicator that my conscious mind frequency has matched my subconscious mind frequency, wherever it is.

Now that I have relaxed myself physically, I going to relax myself mentally. I will program to myself the following information. I am smart, I am creative and I am an achiever. I am smart, I am creative and I am an achiever. I am smart, I am creative and I am an achiever. I can accomplish any goal I want because I know it only takes three to five weeks to make or break a habit. I can accomplish any goal I want because I know it only takes three to five weeks to make or break a habit. I can accomplish any goal I want because I know it only takes three to five weeks to make or break a habit.

I can accomplish any goal. I can accomplish any goal. I can accomplish any goal. First I will see my goal in my mind. I see the goal I would like to accomplish appear in my mind. I see it clearly. I see myself accomplishing this goal. It seems so easy now that I see myself accomplishing it. I visualize this goal being a tremendous success.

I am strong and determined and nothing can stop me from accomplishing this important goal. Now I see all my friends and the people who are important to me standing around me cheering me on. As I look at their faces, I see their support and their pride in me. I feel my own pride fill my body as I'm accomplishing this goal. I truly feel loved.

There is nothing I cannot do if I believe in myself, love myself, and support myself. There is nothing I cannot do if I believe in myself, love myself, and support myself. There is nothing I cannot do if I believe in myself, love myself, and support myself.

I know I can visualize success at any time in my life. As I take another deep breath, I feel as though I am in an even deeper state of relaxation than ever before. I am totally at ease.

I see the light again above my head. It is even more brilliant and whiter than it was before. This light is an energizing light; as it moves through my head, it energizes my head. As it moves through my arms, it energizes my arms. It continues to energize my back, as it moves down my spine. It continues to move down the front of my body into my chest. As I take another deep breath, it energizes my chest and stomach. It moves down my legs, energizing my legs, down into my feet, energizing my feet. Now my whole body is energized in this brilliant energizing white light. I feel more alert and alive than ever before. I feel like there is nothing I cannot accomplish. I feel great about myself and my energy has increased ten times what it was. As I count to five I will gradually reactivate my energized muscles and become more consciously aware of the world around me. On five, I will be fully conscious and wide awake. One...I feel sensation coming back to my body. Two...I am slowly moving my toes around. Three...as I take a deep breath, I come back to feel the presence of the room around me. Four...my whole body feels a new energized sensation. On five, I will be fully conscious alert and feeling great. Five...I am fully conscious, alert and feeling great.

Now, how do you feel? Write down how it felt this time and what the difference was.

_____

_____

_____

_____

Doesn't this prove what happens when you live your life from your alpha state? Every time you have a goal, something you would like to accomplish, listen to the *"Goals"* side of the tape, or have someone read the script to you and see yourself accomplishing it. The goal can be anything you choose it to be. Play it or listen to it over and over again with the same goal in mind.

When you are in the alpha state, you have a clear path to all the information your subconscious wants to give you. When you are in the beta state you turn off access to this information. The negative programming appears and shuts off the path to your subconscious.

The goal is to get back to the alpha state and to stay there.

Since the beta and alpha states cross between ten and fourteen cycles per second, you can be awake and alert and still be in a place of relaxation. This is the place where you will want to live. It is referred to as the alpha/beta state. It's where the conscious and subconscious mind meet, and the "chemistry" is perfect. This state of mind is like walking in a constant state of meditation. This is the state of mind where Jesus, and the great prophets and teachers (like Buddha) have lived. Hey, it worked for them, so my guess is, it will also work for you! Let's get Hacker's opinion.

"OK, so maybe you guys don't care to be a prophet. Would you like to be a great athlete? This is the place where athletes perform their best. It's 'the zone' man. Need I say more?"

The difference in the Olympics or any championship game is often due to the person or team visualizing victory or perfection and staying in their alpha/beta state. I had a friend who played soccer in college. He was an awesome goalie. He said that when he was in the alpha/beta state everything slowed down. He could actually jump up to where the ball was being kicked, before the kick was even completed. The alpha state slows things down. That is why when we are kids, time goes by more slowly. Remember, when you were a small child, how long it used to take until Christmas or until school was out?

"Kimberly...'Forever,' I think, was the answer."

Think about it. When you are about to give a speech in front of a group, what happens? When you are asked to introduce a group of people, on the spot, that you don't know too well, what happens? All right, let's try this one. Have you ever studied for a test and you knew, you knew the information inside and out? You take the test and you get some blocks, but as you leave the room (after having handed in the test) you suddenly remember the answers. The reason this happens is because you are in your beta state. The state of mind where you are well over fourteen cycles per second. You shut off all access to your subconscious information (where all your test information is stored). As you leave the room, you slide back into your alpha/beta state and bingo, the answers miraculously appear.

This also happens when people get into arguments. Have you ever gotten into an argument and thought of all the things you could or should have said...later? The reason is the same. If you want to be at your optimal thinking level, if you want to be mentally quick on your feet, you must be in your alpha/beta state. You must be relaxed. If you want to help yourself get to the alpha state quickly, then take three deep breaths; they will help to relax you.

I have another student, Radcliff, whom I had been teaching tennis for about four weeks. He had progressed quickly because, unlike most people, he has learned to think and stay in his alpha/beta state. He did this by listening to his "Goals" tape over and over again, while inputting visions of the perfect tennis game. He is trying out for his high school tennis team next year. I put odds on Radcliff making the varsity team and having a winning season.

Enough examples, I would really like to challenge you now. Let's look at some things that we know about our brain-wave frequencies and our brains in general.

---

1. We all have them.

2. We use less than 10% of them.

3. We are more powerful than any computer we have created. (This includes televisions, radios, satellites, etc.)

4. We have frequencies in them as do many of the things we have created (televisions, radios, missiles, etc.).

With this information, look at what your brain or anyone's brain is really capable of achieving. Think about it.

Have you ever been thinking about someone and that person called you on the phone? Have you ever felt something good or bad was going to happen to a friend of yours, and it did? Remember, the brain is limitless. Think about its power. What do you think it is capable of achieving?

Listen to this next script by taping it yourself, by having someone else tape it, or by purchasing the actual **EmpowerMind** tape. As I said earlier, it's best to have the scripts taped. This script is entitled "The Wise Person." This tape will bring you into your alpha state and help you answer questions for yourself.

Remember, in the last chapter, you wrote a question to your wise person. Well, it is time to find the answer. When you listen to the tape, you will feel as though you have been experiencing the journey for hours, and it is merely twenty minutes long. You will feel relaxed and refreshed when the tape is over. So, go now, make the tape and listen to it. Remember to speak slowly, clearly and with appropriate voice inflection.

Wise Person Script

Welcome to a journey into relaxation through **EmpowerMind**. Think of a question you would like an answer to in your life. The question can be about school, relationships, family or work. It can be any question. Just gently allow the question to appear in your mind. *(Pause.)*

Now, make sure your arms and legs are uncrossed and that you are in a comfortable position.

Shut your eyes and take a deep breath. *(Pause.)*

This relaxation adventure will naturally match your conscious and subconscious mind frequencies, wherever they are.

I will be speaking in first person. When you hear my voice you will hear it as if it were your own voice talking to yourself.

Now, as I take another deep breath, I imagine a warm soothing white light over my head, relaxing my head. This warm light continues over my forehead, relaxing my forehead, down to my nose, relaxing my nose, down to my lips, relaxing my lips, down to my chin, relaxing my chin, until my whole face is bathed in the soothing white light. *(Pause.)*

The warm soothing light then moves down to my neck, relaxing my neck, it moves down into my shoulders until my shoulders are completely relaxed.

This warm white light moves slowly down from my shoulders into my upper arms, down to my lower arms, then down to my hands and all the way down to my finger tips, until my arms and hands are completely relaxed in this warm soothing white light. *(Pause.)*

The light continues down into my chest. As I take a deep breath and let it out, the light continues to gently glide down my stomach, I feel its warmth. I also notice the light slowly pouring out the back of my neck down my spine, relaxing all the muscles down my spine, one by one, until my back is completely relaxed in the soothing warm white light. *(Pause.)*

I take another deep breath and notice my whole upper body is completely relaxed in this warm soothing white light.

The light continues to move down into my buttocks until they are completely relaxed. It moves down my thighs and down into my calves until my legs are completely relaxed in this soothing white light. Then it moves into my feet, all the way down to my toes until my feet and toes are completely relaxed. Now my whole body is completely relaxed in this warm soothing white light. I slowly move through my body, looking for any tension. If I find tension I simply concentrate on it and say to myself "Relax." *(Pause.)*

As I take a deep breath, I feel relaxed like I never have before. I am aware of some other sensation. It could be warm, tingly or a floating sensation. This is an indicator that my conscious mind frequency has matched my subconscious mind frequency, wherever it is.

Now that I have relaxed myself physically, I going to relax myself mentally. I will program, to myself, the following information. I love to relax, I love to learn, I love to study. I love to relax, I love to learn, I love to study. I love to relax, I love to learn, I love to study.

I am a great learner, I learn quickly and easily. I am a great learner, I learn quickly and easily. I am a great learner, I learn quickly and easily. I can accomplish anything I want because I know it only takes three to five weeks to make or break a habit. I can accomplish anything I want because I know it only takes three to five weeks to make or break a habit. I can accomplish anything I want because I know it only takes three to five weeks to make or break a habit.

Now, I'm going to go off by myself for awhile. I imagine myself being in a place where I feel safe and love being alone in my thoughts. I feel relaxed and secure in this special place. It is a beautiful and peaceful day. I am calm, relaxed and happy to be in my special place. I will be alone and peaceful for awhile. *(Pause for sixty seconds.)*

Now, I'm ready to leave this special place knowing I can return at any time. It's time to move on now.

Knowing that deep breaths add to my relaxation, I will take two deep breaths now and feel the sensation in my body get even stronger. *(Pause.)* I know once again that my conscious mind frequency has matched my subconscious mind frequency, wherever it is. I know once again that my conscious mind frequency has matched my subconscious mind frequency, wherever it is. I know once again that my conscious mind frequency has matched my subconscious mind frequency, wherever it is.

Now, in this even deeper state of relaxation, I will allow the question that I thought of when entering this relaxation to slowly appear. *(Pause.)*

I begin walking down a path in the country as I continue to think about this question. As I walk down this path, I notice a meadow, a beautiful meadow, filled with tall green grass and colorful flowers. As I look further down the path I notice a big, majestic willow tree. Sitting next to the tree is a wise person, a very wise person. This person is here to answer all the questions I could ever have. As I walk toward the tree I feel warmth and love reaching out to welcome me.

As I step into the presence of this wise person, I am totally at ease. I sit down comfortably and take some time to really become aware of this person. *(Pause.)*

I feel safe in this person's presence and I fully trust this person. Now, I ask this wise person my question. I notice how my wise person reacts. My answer may be in words or in a gesture or maybe that I am given something. *(Pause.)*

If I do not understand the answer or if I have another question, I will ask that question now. I will soon have to say good-bye to this wise person, so I should say anything else I want to say before I leave. Now, as I say good-bye to this wise person, I wave to the wise person. As I leave I notice all the details of the path and meadow, so I can return to the meadow whenever I wish. I'm thinking of the answer to my question as I leave this meadow and come back to this room. *(Pause.)*

I am finished with my relaxation programming for today. I will gradually reactivate my relaxed muscles and become more consciously aware of the world around me. One, I feel sensation coming back to my body. Two, I am slowly moving my toes around. Three, I am slowly moving my neck and shoulders. Four, I am slowly taking in a deep breath and feeling the presence of this room around me. Now, on five, I will be fully conscious alert and feeling great. Five, I am fully conscious alert and feeling great.

Well, what did you think? It was amazing, wasn't it? Did you get your question answered? What did the wise person say or do? Write it down.

_____

_____

_____

_____

"Hey! Kimberly, you forgot something. What if they didn't get an answer? If you didn't get an answer the first time you tried, that's cool, man. You may need to either make your question clearer or it may just take you a few times to get your answer. It took me three times of listening to Kimberly's tape to get my answer. And...I finally got it and...I listened to it and...she went out on a date with me! This stuff really works, so stick with it!"

Thanks again, Hacker!

You have the ability to use your homemade tape or this script anytime you want to get answers for yourself. This tape brings you into the alpha state of mind. It is pretty great, isn't it? Wouldn't it be nice to live in this state of mind all the time? You need to listen to the tape for three to five weeks, because it takes that long to make or break a habit. YES! It takes three to five weeks to make or break a habit. This tape will be a fabulous tool for you. Use it! A student of mine, named Yolanda, used it. She was scared to even read in front of her class. Now, she looks forward to reading in front of groups of people.

Remember, your subconscious cannot tell the difference between imagination and reality; therefore, if you listen to the tape long enough, it will program your mind to stay in the alpha state. If you get out of the alpha state in a few months or so, just listen to the tape again and again and again.

If you say something to yourself over and over again, soon your subconscious mind will believe it.

Angel, one of my students, was in her beta state so much that she couldn't even read in front of her class in school. At thirteen, this is traumatic. She listened to the "Wise Person" and "Goals" tape for several weeks in a row. (She has also been through the course several times.) She could not only read in front of her class, now, but she just spoke at a Rotary Club in Sausalito, California. There were sixty men in the audience! She was one of my testimonials, and she was awesome! She learned to stay in her alpha state while she was fully conscious. Again, this is referred to as the alpha/beta state or, as Hacker says, "the zone of learning."

"That's right and this tape is really rad man! It was one of my favorite parts of the whole workshop. I listen to it almost every night. It even helps me sleep, while my subconscious is sucking it all in."

You really need to listen to this tape with the Wise Person and the Goals as often as possible. There are also some fun adventure tapes available, too, just for when you want to escape the world. (See the order form in the back of the book.)

"Don't go for a drink or drugs. Go slap in one of your imagination journey tapes and take off! In fact, take a friend on the ride with you."

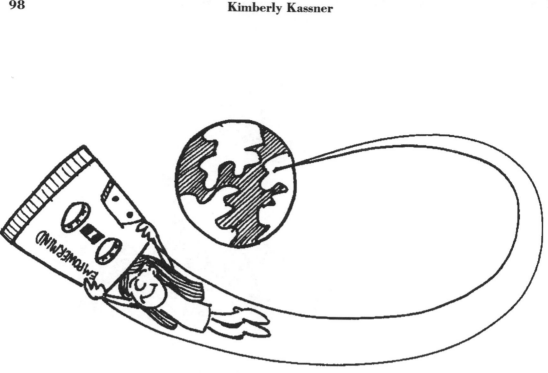

Summary

The alpha state is a state of mind where your mind is moving between seven and fourteen cycles per second. This is the state where you are relaxed, you can tap into subconscious information and you can learn. The beta state is the state of mind where your brain frequencies are moving at ten cycles per second or faster. The beta state is where you are living most of the time. You can change that. If you re-program your mind long enough, you can live in the optimal state of mind: the alpha state and alpha/beta state.

Questions

1. Our brain has brain-wave frequencies. Its ability to communicate is more powerful than man-made inventions with frequencies. Name three of these man-made inventions. _____

   _____

   _____

2. The alpha frequency is between:
   A. 4.5-7.0 cycles per second
   B. 0-18 cycles per second
   C. 7-10 cycles per second
   D. 7-14 cycles per second

3. What brain wave state are people in most of the time?
   A. Alpha
   B. Theta
   C. Sigma Chi
   D. Beta
   E. California

4. What is one way you can get into the alpha state quickly?
   A. Eat sugar
   B. Meditate
   C. Take several deep breaths
   D. Sleep

5. When would you use the "Wise Person" side of the tape? _____

   _____

6. When would you use the "goal" side of the tape? _____

   _____

7. True or False? Brain waves are capable of communicating without spoken words. _____

8. Why is it that you forget names and test answers only moments after you knew them?
   A. Because you are in your alpha state.
   B. Because you are in your beta state.
   C. Because you are in a midwestern state.
   D. It only happens when you are in California

9. What state of mind are athletes in when they accomplish their peak performance?_____

10. Which is your optimal state of performance on a moment to moment basis?
    A. Michigan
    B. Between Oregon and Minnesota
    C. Alpha state
    D. None of the above

Chapter Six

Make Test-Taking Fun

Overview

EmpowerMind skills will help you take tests with pleasure. Have you ever hated, dreaded or panicked over taking tests? If you want to learn how to make taking tests easy and effective, then this is the chapter to read. It shows you how your subconscious and emotions work together, while you are in your alpha state, to help make test taking a *breeze*.

Questions

1. How many steps are there to a taking test?
   A. 10
   B. 11
   C. 6 that really matter
   D. 12
   E. None of the above

2. True or False? You should try to get a previous test from your teacher before taking your test. _____

There are many factors in taking tests. Most of the factors have to do with fear. Do any of these fears sound familar? Fear of: failure, anxiety, not having enough time, trick questions, a test reading like it's in a foreign language, the test making or breaking you, it being the beginning or end of your life... How about the thought 'I think I'm going to die'?'' I'm sure you can think of many more. Do you have anything to add, Hacker?

"Nah, I think you covered the basics..."

The worries are real if you feel them. Once you learn to take tests this new way, those fears should be minimal, if not completely eliminated.

Simply follow the following steps to taking a test. In fact, you may have some that I haven't even mentioned. I hope so!

Step One: ***Study the*** **EmpowerMind** ***techniques for studying.*** Do it the EmpowerMind way. This includes, of course, talking with the teacher personally. See if your teacher will give you a past test, from previous chapters, to study if you promise to return it. Ask the teacher, "What should I focus on in this test?" Let the teacher know it is really important for you to learn this and do well in your class. Teachers love that, and it will help! Trust me, that's how I got through college.

Step Two: ***Review all the information for the test the night before.*** Why? Because your subconscious can work on it all night, while you sleep.

Step Three: ***Listen to your*** **EmpowerMind** ***tape, on the "Goals" side, the night before your test and, as you are drifting into slumber, remind yourself how great you will do on your test the next day.***

Step Four: ***The first thing you say to yourself when you wake up, is that you love tests, and you especially love the one you are going to take, and do so well on, today.***

Step Five: ***Go to class. Take a few deep breaths before the exam to relax.*** (Maybe even add, "I am going to kick some butt on this test today." This is optional of course.)

Step Six: ***Read through the test once.*** If, by chance, a question comes up that you are positive you have the right answer for, then answer it. If you don't know for sure, then skip it and move on. Why do you skip it? Because:

1. You want to build your self confidence.

2. You want to reinforce your alpha state.

3. Your subconscious can work on the ones you skipped, while you are consciously reading the new questions.

4. Sometimes, there are answers toward the end of the test, or triggers that will help you answer one of the questions you passed, so when you go back to it later you will know the answer. Does this make sense or *what?*

Step Seven: ***Go through the test a second time and do this again.*** If you get the answer right away, go for it. If you don't, then don't answer it.

Step Eight: **Go** ***through the test a third time and really think about the answer this time.*** Think about if you learned it in class or from the book. If it was one or the other, think about when or where you learned it. If you still can't get it, then skip it.

Step Nine: *Shut your eyes, concentrate on the time the teacher talked about this question. If you can't get the time, then mentally walk up to the teacher and ask him or her the question.* Whatever the teacher answers in your mind is the right answer. Mark it on the test. Your percentage of correct answers will be higher than just guessing.

Step Ten: *Re-read your test for any silly mistakes.* Make sure your name is on it (I used to forget this one all the time). Make sure you carefully re-read each question. Look for the words "*always*" and "*never.*" Make sure all questions are answered.

Step Eleven: *Hand it in and pat yourself on the back because you did the best you could.*

Step Twelve: If you felt you knew the material and you did poorly on the test, *ask your teacher if you can take an essay test next time. If it was an essay test, ask if you can take a multiple choice test.* My professors in college even let me take multiple choice tests and write the reason *why* I chose the answer on the back. If my answer was wrong, but my reason was right, they would give me credit. *See, teachers can be very supportive!*

If you follow these steps and do not get amazing results, then please write to me and let me know what happened, because it will be the first time. Go out there and take some tests—*and do it with pleasure!*

Summary

Taking tests can become easy if you simply study the EmpowerMind way, stay in your alpha state and let your subconscious do all the work. Oh, and of course, there is always making sure you have communicated with your teachers effectively about how to test you best.

Questions

1. How many steps are there to a taking test?
   A. 10
   B. 11
   C. Six that really matter
   D. 12
   E. None of the above

2. True or False? You should try to get a previous test from your teacher before taking your test? _____

3. Why do you skip questions when taking a test?
    A. So your subconscious can work for you
    B. So you relax
    C. So you can find triggers
    D. So you can find the answers IN the test
    E. All of the above

4. What is the overall reason people hate taking tests?_____
   _____

5. List seven of the test-taking techniques.

    1. _____

    2. _____

    3. _____

    4. _____

    5. _____

    6. _____

    7. _____

Using Positive Attitudes for Personal Power

Overview

This is the favorite lesson of most of my students. It is also one of the most entertaining and powerful chapters in this book. You will learn to create magic in your life by learning to live in the moment more. Make sure you practice these examples. They will bring the meaning of "*fun*" into your life, in a way that even you haven't imagined.

Questions

1. What is the greatest cause of taking the magic out of learning?
    A. Negative programming
    B. Ego
    C. Teachers
    D. Parents
    E. Tests

2. Who affects our attitudes about learning?
    A. Parents
    B. Teachers
    C. Peers
    D. All of the above

3. Why is it,that a teacher can say something negative to two students and one student will be challenged by it, while the other one will become depressed and feel hopeless?
    A. Because some kids are more stupid than others
    B. Because everyone has a different association base, which is based on their past experience

  C. Because some kids are just overly emotional and really need to loosen up their crummy attitudes
  D. This is a lie. If a teacher says something negative, it can only de-motivate the student.
  E. None of the above

4. The magic happens when we live in the _____ .

5. What happens when you act silly? Naturally you begin to _____ and have more _____ .

6. What can you do to make yourself laugh or feel better when you are crying?
  A. Remember there are people who are worse off than you
  B. Read a joke
  C. Do some homework
  D. Look at yourself in the mirror

Why is it that when we are small children we are imaginative, innovative and positive, then something happens and many of us start to lose our zest for life? You may even become distrustful, cynical and filled with fear. For some the magic seems to end.

Be silent for a moment.

It is in our own silence that we discover. We discover who we are versus thinking of who we "should" become. It is the person you are in this moment who is precious, not the imaginary image of the happy person you think you will become in the future. It is in this moment of silence you may discover that person exists within you now.

Do you remember, in the beginning of the book, when I had you shut your eyes and remember what it was like playing and learning when you were three or four years old? You probably had a positive association to playing and learning at that age. Do you know what has happened to you personally that has taken away the magic of learning? Together, we are going to explore what happened to you, and why learning has lost its magic.

You see, as I said in the chapter on the conscious and subconscious mind, you start out as a blank computer, just wanting to be loved, nourished and supported. Then, along the way, you may get some negative programming. The first few years of your life you constantly hear the words "No!" "Don't!" "Get out of there!" "Bad girl!" "Bad boy!" "Stop it!" Children can generally block these negative phrases out, and even the tension their parents feel in their lives, for about three to five years. But then, they begin to believe their limitations, and the programming sticks. Has this happened to you?

Then, you go off into the world of *school*. This is the place where you get teased, picked on, bullied, or sometimes humiliated by classmates or teachers. It is then you begin to lose the magic. You begin to live in fear.

> **"Kimberly, I can totally relate to that. I got picked on when I moved to a new elementary school. Kids were mean to me just because I was new."**

Yeah, Hacker, I know the feeling. Teachers can be that way, too. I remember back in third grade I was very inquisitive, and was always seeking someone's approval. Our teacher, Ms. Opliegh, always got mad if we left the record player on. So, one day, as we were getting ready to move into a circle for our geography lesson, I noticed that the record player was on. I would have gone directly over to shut it off, but I knew the rules about not getting out of our seats (and was proud of it). I simply told Ms. Opliegh that the record player was playing. She either didn't hear me, or she was ignoring me. I, being the persistent child that I was, assumed she didn't hear me. So I raised my hand during the geography lesson. She called on me and I told her, "The record player is playing." I had a good feeling that I was following the rules and helping out. Ms. Opliegh, however, thought differently. She walked up to me, slapped me in the face and said, "OK class, tell Kim that the record player is playing." All together the class repeated, "Kim, the record player is playing." I was devastated! I completely tuned out the rest of the day. (I attribute my poor geography to this incident.) I told my parents immediately when I came home and they were irate! (They were irate at *Ms. Opliegh*, thank goodness.) If they hadn't supported me, I would have been devastated. They had a meeting with her and the principal. Ms. Opliegh didn't bother me again; she just ignored me. She did many cruel things to children. (This was a parochial school, and she was fired at the end of the year.) I know there are many teachers who are awesome, as I have mentioned and will mention again. I have had some who have been incredible examples and mentors in my life. I'm sure that you will, too, if you give them a chance. Unfortunately, there are also a few who are like Ms. Opliegh. They can contribute to your self-esteem or to your lack of it. They help you define your association base.

Sometimes the things parents and teachers do are subtle, and we don't even notice the negative messages we are receiving. Here's another example. One boy who got up in front of his class of peers to give a speech was told by his teacher, during the speech, that he obviously hadn't prepared for this talk. He really had prepared, and when his classmates laughed at him he was humiliated and devastated. Because of that humiliating incident, he lost all his confidence in speaking to groups. He had to give a speech to graduate, and he almost didn't do it. I helped him re-program his negative experience before even working with him on a speech.

He finally got enough confidence to give the speech, but it will be a long time before he feels comfortable giving one.

You see, it's not just the events that create our fears and negative attitudes, it's how we interpret them and what we do about them. Everyone is different. Everyone has different filters, thus producing different association bases. For example, when Louise, a friend of mine, took Speech 101 at Central Michigan University, she had already formed her basic filters and association bases. When her speech teacher gave her a C on a speech that everyone in her class raved about and that she was very proud of, she took it as a challenge in her life. She knew it was the professor's issue. Professor Pedesco wanted her to stand behind the podium and not move. Louise got too connected with the audience, according to Professor Pedesco. Her filter interpreted it to her as, "You just wait, Susan Pedesco, when I am a famous public speaker, you will be sorry." Like, Professor Pedesco would even care either way. The point is, Louise's filters and association base were for the most part already formed. What do you think would have happened if that had happened to her in second grade?

Think about what information you have received in your life that has created your negative association to learning and has taken the fun and delight out of your life. It's time to turn that around with some new "Self-talk."

What do I mean when I say the words Self-talk? Self-talk is "what you say when you talk to yourself." (No, it is not when you have lost your mind.) Whatever you put into your mind is whatever comes out in your actions. If you tell yourself negative things about yourself, then negative things will come out. You create your own reality. If you think the world stinks, then guess what? It stinks. If you think the world is a magical, beautiful place, then guess what? It is a magical, beautiful place. You bring into your life the things which reflect who you are. Everyone you bring into your life is a mirror of you.

So often students say, "But, my friends are so...well, they are negative and have such low self-esteem." They go on to tell me how rotten their friends are to them. My first question is, "How are these friends reflecting you?" Well, think about it in your life—how do your friends reflect you? Don't try to change your friends, try to change yourself, then you'll have space for the new friends that you will attract into your life.

"Kimberly, I really need to share this with my peers out there. What you're saying really hit home for me. Two years ago, when I took EmpowerMind, I realized that I had loser friends 'cuz I was pretty much of a loser myself. (I hate to admit that.) Once I changed, my friends changed. It sounds like bunk, but it really worked."

Now please write the five main characteristics of your closest friends.

1. _____

2. _____

3. _____

4. _____

5. _____

Now, look at these closely, in the silence and safety of your own room, and ask yourself, "Which of those five traits are really me?" You will get some good answers about what traits you should keep and which ones you should throw away.

No matter what you think, **no one is an island.** Everyone affects everyone in one way or another. We all give off energy, negative and positive, to those around us. Does this sound like California mish-mosh? Well, let me ask you, have *you* ever walked into a room with nobody even talking and you could "feel" the tension? Have you ever walked into a room and felt happiness, love, excitement and cheer?

You see; you are not an island. If you can raise your self-esteem by changing your self-talk into positive self-talk or by doing nice things for yourself, you can help change the world. You will be coming in contact with thousands, possibly millions, of people throughout your lifetime. If you have good energy and a positive attitude inside, you will have it outside, too. This will affect the people who come in contact with you, just like you are affected when you walk into a positive or negative environment. So, go try it. See if it works. Notice the energy of the rooms you walk into and if it's negative, try to change it. Many people who are very negative, promote more negative energy.

Melanie, a girl from one of my classes, shared with us how she changed people's attitudes when she flew on an airplane. Melanie continually tests her ability to change energy in her environment. When a whole line of people got cranky (this happens a lot when planes are delayed), she smiled and started telling pilot jokes. A few people started to laugh and loosen up. Soon, the whole line was feeling better about the delay. Positive energy is contagious. So, go out and try it! Spread some positive energy. The world needs *you!* You will help the magic begin.

Now, you may be asking, "How do you get self-esteem, other than just telling yourself how great you are (and meaning it) and sending out positive energy?" Well, I have a few more ideas (out of many) to share with you. So often we concentrate on the negative things that we do in a day, rather than the positive.

Think about this one: Have you ever participated in a sport and concentrated afterwards on all the things you did wrong, instead of the things you did right? Or, you just met the girl or guy you've been dying to meet all year. All you can think about is all the dumb things you said or did, instead of the smart things you said or did? Does this one sound familiar? Hey, it's reinforced in our lives all the time. The media prints all the bad, not the good, and even your teachers tell you how many you got "*wrong*," not how many you got "right." It's a natural thing to remind ourselves how we screwed up, so I'd like you to start this new way of thinking by writing down ten positive things about yourself.

An example might be, "I'm a good listener for my friends."

OK, your turn.

1. _____

2. _____

3. _____

4. _____

5. _____

6. _____

7. _____

8. _____

9. _____

10. _____

Now, did that hurt? Re-read it. Come on, re-read it over and over until you really believe it! This is a good exercise to do at the end of every day. You just write down all the good and positive things you did that day. It will help change your focus from the negative to the positive. When that happens, self-esteem is a natural by-product. Buy or make a journal in which to keep your strengths. This is very powerful.

The next suggestion is called the "Treasure Chest." This is something I devised for myself for whenever I feel like—like the scum of the earth: the fungus among us. I have a special box where I keep all my positive momentos from my friends: letters, thank-you cards, past achievements, funny and happy pictures, poems, love letters and anything else that makes me feel good about myself and what I have done.

This is what I would like you to do. Keep your own treasure chest. When you are feeling low, you can go to a private place and open up your own personal treasure box. You can re-read all the wonderful things about you. If you don't have anything to put in it yet, then put in the list of strengths you just wrote about yourself. This will be a beautiful start. As the years go by, it will fill up. If it doesn't, it doesn't mean you are a bad person, it simply means you just need to give more to others.

Here comes another big secret. Would you like to know when the magic comes in your life? The magic comes when you learn to *live in the moment*. "Living in the moment" means you have to eliminate your association base entirely. If you don't, you automatically attach things that aren't real to a situation.

Have you ever taken a spontaneous trip? Have you ever had a spontaneous evening? (If you haven't, you'd better go start!) Did you have fun? I'm talking like major rad time! If you had the same experience and you'd planned it, it wouldn't be half as much fun. Why? Think about it.

It is because you had expectations! You were expecting it to be a certain way, based on your past experience. However, if you do something new and spontaneous, you have no expectation, and you have no past association base from your planning. It is times like these, that you *live in the moment and the magic definitely happens!*

I think it's time for another mission. Oh yes! It is time. This is really going to be a stretch for you to not only live in the moment, but relish the moment. Next time you are in a traffic jam (you know how much we all love traffic jams), turn up the music and sing! Sing your little brains out! Make up a song if you need to.

Don't give up faith in the special magic that you are learning you already have!

Just sing and get into the beat. Or, imagine yourself, fifty years from now, like one of the Jetsons. You see yourself flying over all the cars. "Beam me up, Scottie," is another favorite among my students. I don't care if you're an adult or a child. If you want to change your mood and the situation, you have to be silly. We truly seem to lose being silly, creating laughter and having fun. You don't see three- and four-year-olds getting uptight about a traffic jam, do you? They know they can't do anything about it. Let's learn from them and *loosen up!*

When you act silly, you can't help but laugh (often at yourself, but that's OK). I have been singing and laughing so much, at myself, that I start smiling at the people around me. They may think I'm nuts, but guess what? They generally start smiling back. The frowns and the tension of the people in the cars around me fade.

Silliness has power. A positive attitude can change people. Most importantly, positive attitudes can change you! Next time you or one of your parents want to merge into a lane, in the midst of a traffic jam, have them wave and smile to the person they are cutting in front of, and you will be amazed at the response. Not only will the other car let you in without a problem, but they will smile back at you. Smiling sends off a chemical reaction in your body that "naturally" makes you feel better, whether you like it or not. So smile as much as possible. You will also change the mood of those around you.

Do you have anything to add Hacker?

"Hey, make funny faces in front of the mirror. You can't help but laugh at how ridiculous you are. A great time to do this is when you are upset and crying. (Do I sound demented? That's OK, it's all part of being an EmpowerMind graduate.) Just go in front of that mirror and look at how funny you look. It always makes me laugh. It may do the same for you. You may start crying again, but looking in the mirror can keep the problem or emotion in perspective."

You may have one hundred ideas on how you can bring more positive attitudes and fun into your life. I hope you do but, even more importantly, I hope you use them. It's great to have ideas but, if you don't *practice* them or use them, they are meaningless. I'd rather you have only one idea of how to bring positive attitudes and fun into your life, and use it, than have a hundred that you never use.

You have to start somewhere, so begin with the traffic jam. If you never seem to be in a traffic jam, try it when you are in long lines. This could be at the cafeteria, at the store, in a bank, etc. Use your imagination! Sometimes, I imagine that everyone in the line is a future student of mine. I look them over and fantasize how they would be standing on chairs screaming and laughing, like in the workshop. Or, I may imagine them all (even the women) in boxer shorts, or they are all spies hired by...my parents, or they are all movie stars undercover, or aliens from another planet. They all entertain me and make me laugh. You can make life be however you want it to be, so create your own reality and *imagine, imagine, imagine!*

Through your imagination, you can even use this positive attitude technique to avoid pain. When I go running, at some point the running becomes painful (generally two or three steps out the door!). It is at this time that I use a positive

attitude. I run around a canyon with hills, streams, waterfalls and redwoods. I imagine cartoon characters coming out of the woods and running with me. Oh yes, Dumbo, Bugs Bunny, Goofy and even Mickey Mouse. Sometimes, if it gets real bad, I imagine angels swooping me up and carrying me up the hill. That is easy to visualize because there are rays of light pouring through the redwoods. I have even, admittedly, imagined the man of my dreams, around the next corner, begging me to run just a little longer. If that isn't incentive, I don't know of any! So, try using a positive attitude in all areas of your life.

Now, let's look at another way you produce self-esteem or a lack of it. I'm going to give you an example. Then, I'm going to share some true stories about what has happened in the lives of some students and adults I know. You decide, based on their stories, what kind of person you would like to be. It's up to you, but then again, it always is.

OK, you are told, right from childhood, that you are a good athlete or student. So, one day, you have a bad game. In fact, the team loses because you played so badly. Or, you have a big final exam and you flunk it. Odds are you will feel bad, but your self-esteem won't be defined because your past experience, your association base, will reinforce the event that just happened and put it into perspective. But, if you were a crummy athlete or a crummy student and you played well in a sport or got an "A" on a final, you might feel great and it might give you a boost, but you would most likely feel it was just luck. You'd had too much personal experience to know otherwise.

An acquaintance of mine was going out with my house mate and me. We were meeting three guys, none of whom we were dating or had ever dated. (My friend had a mad crush on one of them). The guy she had a crush on couldn't make it. She took it personally. He had to work on a special project and couldn't get out of work. This wasn't even a date; it was a get-together with friends. She took it personally because her association base said, "I like him; therefore, he should feel the same way. If he doesn't show up, it's a direct reflection on me, not the rest of the group. It has to do with him not liking me, because if he really liked me, he would have been there." When I tried to explain that sometimes employees can't leave work, her reply was, "I can always get off of work, so that's no excuse." See, she came only from her own experience. She had brought expectations into the evening and was living in her past experience, not in the moment. Her own self-esteem was based on her negative reinforcement of the past.

When you learn to live in the moment, the past doesn't matter. It can guide you, of course, but it is not your present reality. This does not mean you should go into the ghetto and hang out wearing a miniskirt (especially if you're a guy), carrying $500 dollars on you, to test this. I'm not ruling out common sense and your intelligence, in the present moment. I am, however, asking you to live in the moment, try new things and take more risks.

One of my friends, Jack, was telling me the other day about some of his high school experiences. He said that he was on a championship baseball team in Detroit. His wife threw in, "He was also the star running-back in his football league." He had school status, but most importantly he had self-esteem, because he constantly took risks and believed in himself. He said he never really cared about peer pressure.

One day, Jack decided to join the high school choir. ("Oh my gosh, what a wimp," seemed to be a popular reaction to guys joining the choir.) Well, all the students thought, in the past, that choir was for girls and sissies. Jack joined simply because he liked to sing. He tried things because he wanted to try them, not because he wanted to be in the "in-group." After he joined the choir, several of the other football players joined. The other guys had thought about it, but were too scared about what people would say. Jack was a leader, and he still is a leader; he is currently a medical doctor. You can be a leader, too. Being a leader is about listening to *your* heart, not everyone else's. It's about doing what you *know* is the right thing to do. You are the only one who can decide what will make you happy and successful. Sometimes, when you do this, other people will even follow your lead. Maybe that's all they are waiting for is for you to take the lead, *so get out there, live in the moment and be a leader. The world needs you!*

When Jennifer broke up with a boyfriend in high school, she was devastated. Every time she had a challenge, she would think of him. "I'll show him!" She would say to herself. "He'll be sorry we broke up when he sees what I have accomplished and who I have become." I'm sure he wouldn't have cared either way, but it helped her face and work through her challenges. It was her incentive. Instead of losing her self-esteem, she was gaining more self-esteem. You can make even painful situations turn out positive for yourself, depending on what filter you use when the information comes through to you.

These are just a few examples of what can happen in everyday life. You will learn some practical application of this to your school or work life, in the chapter on "How Do You Learn?" Until then, start practicing in your everyday life. Make your life a magical adventure by creating your own association base—your own reality. If you create a positive reality for yourself, life will become that way and self-esteem will be a natural by-product.

Creating your own reality can back-fire but, when it does, you may learn a valuable lesson. I did. Once this back fired on me because I went too far and lost my sense of compassion for people who weren't exactly like me. When I taught the Dale Carnegie Course, I used to be Ms. Happy, all the time. It wasn't always real, though. It is important to experience your feelings in a healthy way, no matter what they are, and to be truthful about them. I took my positive attitude to an extreme. I used to feel a positive attitude was everything. I expected everyone else to be this way, too. It always seems I get a lesson when I am insensitive and not real. I've noticed the universe has a beautiful sense of humor.

Here's an example of creating my own reality (not by choice) and seeing what can happen. One day I was feeling a little down and a friend called and really cheered me up.

I got rejuvenated. I threw on some jeans and a T-shirt, and headed down Chestnut Street, into San Francisco, to get my haircut. I was on top of the world! I passed a few guys and they waved with big smiles on their faces. They screamed out "HEEEELLLLLO!" I said hello back and just thought, "Wow! I look terrible, so I know they must feel my positive attitude—my positive energy is showing." (I mean it was *everything*, wasn't it)?...Or so I thought. I really felt great. I walked on a little further and there were some construction workers working. One stopped, nudged a friend and with huge smiles they yelled, "Good Morning!" Well, it was music to my ears, and by this time I was flying! I floated to the hair salon. I got to the door, saw my reflection in the window, and noticed my zipper was *wide open!* So, sometimes, things are not as they seem.

It is important to realize some people's attitudes are due to a lot of pain and that they are not trying to be mean. We get lessons presented to us all the time.

It's just our paying attention to them which is important. Sometimes, we create our own reality and it has *nothing* to do with what is actually happening.

You know, from early childhood, we are trained not to take risks, but rather to be fearful of risks and play it safe. (Do you doubt this? Maybe you overcame this fear of risks, but the programming starts early.) Have you ever had your mom tell you, before you left the house, "Make sure you go out and take a lot of risks today honey? Go out and try the impossible, stretch yourself, do something you have never done before!" OK, I made my point. Instead we are told, "Be careful. Watch yourself. Be good." (Boy, is that vague!) We are taught to repress our creativity and imaginations at an early age. Much of our creativity and imagination have been repressed and have been substituted for fear. Many of us don't even realize how deeply fear has been ingrained. Many young people are scared to simply be themselves.

Teenagers are the future of this world. In fact, I prefer working with teenagers. Why? Because, the older the people are, in the **EmpowerMind** workshops, the more shut-down their imagination tends to be. Teenagers have great imaginations. I'd put my money on your imagination any day. This is only a general rule of course. Some adults have the natural inner strength to ignore outside influences and recognize their gifts. These people are still child-like and many are creative geniuses, doing what they love for a living.

Reverend Fred Johnson was in one of my workshops. He was so filled with love for what he was doing, that he could hardly contain his enthusiasm. I frequented his church, in Marin City, and I have never seen a pastor live his life with such pure passion. He gets so excited when he preaches that he loses track of time. (About dinner time, he notices the congregation passing out!) He is truly using his gifts. Wow! Think about how different the world would be, if everyone, like Reverend Johnson, loved their job!

Why do you think that approximately 95% of the people in the United states are not passionate about their jobs (according to a *New York Times* study)? Think about this question a minute before reading on. In fact, write down three reasons:

1. _____

2. _____

3. _____

Here are some of the reasons students have come up with in my class:

1. They took the job because of the money.
2. They took the job because they never went to college.
3. They took the job because everyone else in their family did.
4. They took the job because their family didn't approve of it, even if they really didn't like it. (Rebellion)
5. They were afraid of failing.
6. They were afraid of succeeding. Success felt uncomfortable and involved a lot of responsibility.
7. They were never encouraged or supported in doing what they were good at.
8. They had low self-esteem.

These are just to name a few. There are hundreds of reasons (oops, I mean excuses). Some kids never even find out what they are good at, or if they do, they are told, "That's just for fun," or "You won't make any money at that," or "You are really better suited for..." It is important to find out what you're good at doing, and then become 100% committed to it. Unfortunately, many of us don't know how to find out what our gifts are. Would you like to find out? OK, then complete this next exercise.

1. What makes you excited to get up in the morning? (It's OK if it's something fun like: a weekend to play, an athletic event, a party, going to the beach, etc. Just write it down.) _____

_____

_____

2. Now, what part of that event or enjoyable time is the most exciting for you? What moment do you feel happiest? (Example: If you like to put on parties, ask yourself, "Is it doing the dishes that turns me on?" — *Not*. Is it being with friends? Is it being the center of attention? Is it making the invitations? Is it feeling loved? What specific moment are you most turned on when doing this?) _____

_____

_____

Every time you look forward to something in school or even an assignment in school, fill out this question in your mind. What really turns you on? If you learn this now, you will save yourself a lot of grief; you'll learn what to do that will make you happy for the rest of your life. Sometimes, it will seem so natural and easy to you that you won't be able to imagine making a living at it someday. But you will, in some way.

There was a boy who played with trucks, collected trucks—in fact, all he seemed to get truly excited about was trucks. Everyone was sure he'd be a failure because he would always be a child interested in trucks. Well, that's what they thought until he created one of the wealthiest trucking companies in the world!

I used to get sent out in the hall constantly for talking as a child. (Can you imagine that?) I was always talking and distracting people. I never in my wildest dreams imagined that people would start to listen. I never dreamed I would be speaking for a living and getting paid good money for it. It is so true what the books say: "Do what you love and the money will follow." Just imagine what this world would be like if everyone did what they loved? So, this is your first step. Get in touch with what you love. If you can't come up with anything, then you need to experiment with new things more. Get involved in acting, a new sport, a meditation class or become a camp counselor. You won't discover what you love unless you get yourself out there and experiment.

Now, once you figure out what you really love to do (which may change in years to come, by the way), then you need to move on to step two: *Commitment.* You have to be 100% committed to your dream. If you are less than 100% committed, then outside influences can destroy your vision, your dream. If you are only 95% committed and your mom or dad or a best friend tells you, "You're nuts. Do you know how hard it is to make money being an artist or cartoonist?" Or, "You want to be a surfer-lifeguard? What a waste. Only lazy people do that!" Or, "You want to be an actress? Do you know how slim your chances are?" Well, if you hear this stuff from enough people you care about, your 95% will slide down to 70%...and then further, until you lose sight of your dream altogether.

Whatever you do, if you are less than 100% committed, do not (*I repeat, do not*) share your dream with anyone who may even have a slight chance of negatively influencing you. Because if you do, you will lose your strength. Share your dream with people who will believe in you, people who believe in miracles. This is critical! If you ignore this step, you'll be doomed. You have to be 100% committed before you can share your vision with people who won't support you. I didn't even tell

my parents I was starting my business until two months after I had made the decision. (I waited until I was 100% committed). When I did tell them, I heard every reason why it wouldn't work, and that I should get a *real* job. At that point it didn't matter, because...what do you think? Yes! I was 100% committed! If I hadn't been, you wouldn't be reading this book right now.

What else can you do to affirm your commitment? Well, you can do hundreds of things. Write your overall dream down. Draw it, or put pictures of positive role models, who are living your dream, on your mirror and look at them every morning. Do research and find out how other people succeeded at your dream. Spend time volunteering with those people to learn more about it and get your foot in the door. Remember, this is your dream and you can put in all the free time it takes to make it happen. If there's a will, there is always a way. If you get stuck, go to someone you know will support you and help you find a solution. Most importantly, always remember, *You can do it!* My dad always told me, if you're going to use your imagination and dream, *dream big*; there are no limits to your imagination.

The third way to make sure you reach your dreams and become 100% committed is to never, I mean never, give up! Life is nothing if you lose your dreams. Let's see if you can guess who this person is who never gave up.

- He had a miserable marriage.
- He lost three children, ages four, eleven and eighteen.

- He failed at business, not once but twice.

- He suffered a nervous breakdown. (Geez, even I might have given up at this point).

- He was defeated for:
    Legislature
    Speaker of the House
    Elector
    Senate twice
    Congress twice
    The Vice Presidency

- *And, in 1861, he was elected President of the United States.*

Where would our world be without Abraham Lincoln? Where will our world be without you? *Don't ever give up!*

The three things that stop us from reaching our goals (eventually) are *fear, fear, and* fear! When you eliminate fear, there is only one thing left. This emotion is the single most important thing in this book and is the one emotion that will create happiness and success in your life. This emotion, which is the opposite of fear, is *love*.

Summary

We start out life as open, loving, little babies. We are excited to learn, we live in the moment and life is magical. Somehow, through our negative parental programming, fears, and our school systems, we lose this magic. We can gain this back again, with re-programming and learning to live in the moment. Life can be magical again. We can learn to laugh and be positive, even in the most negative situations. A positive attitude is possible for anyone. We must practice, practice, practice, in order to reinforce positive attitudes daily and be 100% committed to living our dream.

Questions

1. What is the greatest cause of taking the magic out of learning?
   A. Negative programming
   B. Ego
   C. Teachers
   D. Parents
   E. Tests

2. Who affects our attitudes about learning?
   A. Parents
   B. Teachers
   C. Peers
   D. All of the above

3. Why is it that a teacher can say something negative to two students, and one student will be challenged by it, while the other one will become depressed and feel hopeless?
   A. Because some kids are more stupid than others
   B. Because everyone has a different association base, based on their past experience
   C. Because some kids are just overly emotionally and really need to loosen up their crummy attitudes
   D. This is a lie. If a teacher says something negative, it can only demotivate the student
   E. None of the above

4. The magic happens when we live in the _____ .

5. What happens when you act silly? Naturally you begin to _____ and have more _____ .

6. What can you do to make yourself laugh or feel better when you are crying?
   A. Remember there are worse people off than you
   B. Read a joke
   C. Do some homework
   D. Look in the mirror at yourself

7. True or False? You can use your imagination to avoid pain. _____

8. True or False? Most of us are trained at any early age to take risks. _____

9. Approximately _____ % of all people in the United States are not passionate about their jobs.
   A. 25%
   B. 50%
   C. 95%
   D. 69

10. What happens when we learn to live in the moment? _____

    _____

    _____

    _____

11. Do what you love and the _____ will follow.

12. If you are less than_____ % committed; you have a great chance of failing.
    A. 20%
    B. 100%
    C. 95%
    D. 85%

13. When the book refers to your "treasure chest" it means:
    A. A chest filled with money
    B. You working out, weight lifting, to build a big chest
    C. A chest filled with positive memories about you
    D. A chest filled with positive self-esteem books

14. Self-talk means:
    A. What you say when you talk to yourself
    B. You have pushed this positive attitude stuff too far
    C. When someone else talks to you and you believe it
    D. None of the above

15. True or False? You create your own reality. _____

    Before you read on, please take a break; you deserve one!

Robert Rabbin, a great philosopher, personal mentor and dear friend, has eloquently captured the essence of love. I have taken a few key phrases from "The Drunkenness of Love" to share with you. It's the highest "high" you can ever reach. It's within you in this moment.

> *Love is never absent from our lives. We do not have to find it. We are it. The problem is not that we don't know how to love, or whom to love in what way. The problem is that we are afraid of love, because it consumes us....*

> *Love is not infatuation, excitement, or hopeful anticipation. Love is an inner ecstasy, an intoxication, a drunkenness. Love is the soft music that flows from life itself. Love is friendly to everyone. Love joins us together and connects us to everything. Love knows no fear or hurt. Love wants nothing because it is in itself full and complete. In this love there is no seeking love. In this love we know we are love. We feel this love flow from our veins to the farthest galaxies and back again. In silence, we know that we are love: our core is love. Love is within us.*

Chapter Eight

Emotions — The Power They Give You

Overview

The information in this chapter alone has created miracles. It has not only helped students get better grades and make school more fun, but it has virtually saved lives and helped people soar beyond what they had believed were their limits. You will begin to understand that without *love* life is a big *zero!* You will even learn secrets about your teachers. I suggest you read this chapter a few times. It is by far, the most important one in this book.

Questions

1. True or False? There are only two kinds of emotions. _____
2. _____ is the most powerful negative emotion and _____ is the most powerful emotion of all.
3. True or False? It is more powerful to forgive than to get revenge. _____
4. Life - Love = _____

"I'm so excited for you! This is Kimberly's best chapter yet!"

Emotions, how will they play a part in your learning process? There are negative and positive emotions. Most people primarily live in the negative ones, the greatest of these is *fear*. Fear is very strong. In fact, I can only think of one emotion greater than fear and that's the one we are going to concentrate on. The emotion greater than fear is simply...Love. We all begin life from a place of love. All we want to do is love and be loved, but then, somehow, fear gets in the way. This is programmed at a very early age.

Love is the most powerful emotion of all. When you set your visions based on love, prosperity is your result. I guess it's a good time to share a simple definition

of love (the way I see it). Genuine love is selfless and unattached to fear. It demands nothing in return (this is where surrender comes in). It is based on the desire for growth and the highest good for whatever focus the love is being poured into. Love draws in more love. It does not "control," it just is. There are no conditions to love, there are no judgments...it just is.

> If I speak in the tongues of men and angels, but have not love, I am a noisy gong or a clanging cymbal. And if I have prophetic powers, and understand all mysteries and all knowledge, and if I have all faith, so as to remove mountains, but have not love, I am nothing. If I give away all I have, and if I deliver my body to be burned, but have not love, I gain nothing.

1 Corinthians 13:1-3

With love *anything is possible!*

Why is love the most powerful emotion of all? The best way to explain this is to give you examples and you can decide. Do you remember the movie, *The Karate Kid?* The master, Myogi, was challenged to fight the head trainer of the karate school. The head trainer was the challenger and wanted to fight, while the master chose *not* to fight. Who do you think was the most powerful? Did this person come from a place of love or hate, anger or compassion? Is it more powerful to forgive someone who has really gone too far and upset you? Or, is it more powerful for you to seek revenge on this person? If we had more love in this world, we would have more people who loved their careers and each other. Do you think this would result in a more powerful or less powerful world? If we had more love, we'd have fewer wars...you decide.

The power of love is proven in relationships all the time. If someone gets angry at you and you hold anger or hate toward that person, then you lose your power. If you simply send love to the person, instead of hate or anger, then you won't carry that negative feeling around with you all day. You will actually gain more power, knowing that the person cannot and will not "get to you." If the person can affect you, that person has the power, not you. Think about when you get in a fight or if you have seen someone else in a fight. Which person is more powerful? Is it the one who lashes out, screams, or physically hurts the other person or is it the person who walks away, loves, and forgives? You decide.

> "I really feel I need to comment on this. This happens in school all the time. People get so 'bent out' for no reason. It really makes ya' take notice when someone is calm and just walks away. I mean, it makes 'em look pretty cool, like they're really powerful or something."

Here's a simple equation that I think you'll figure out on your own.

$$\text{Life - Love} = \underline{\hspace{3cm}}.$$

What do you think? Imagine people who have no love in their lives. These are the people who end up in pain and anger. The pain and anger is so great that often they just explode. Many times, these people take a lot of innocent people along with them. Many people in gangs have little or no love in their lives. They tend to join gangs as a substitute for the love they do not have. They want a sense of family, so they go to a place where they feel they will get it. They try to substitute real love by joining gangs, but it never works. Joining gangs just creates more pain for themselves and others. It's the same with many of the people on the streets. Without love, life is nothing worthwhile. Life - Love = *Zero, a big zero!* The people who cannot give or receive love in this world are *big zeros!* I know that person won't be you!

So, if you have little to no love in your life, how can you get it? How could you possibly make people love you? Could you force them or threaten them?

"NOT!"

You can, however, learn to be a friend and send a lot of love out into the world. Get involved in a project; volunteer your time. Help an old person across the street, baby-sit for free, mow an elderly person's lawn, make cookies for a neighbor, etc. Be creative! Send love out to the people you come in contact with everyday, and I can guarantee that someone will send it back. Whatever you do, don't give up! Love for you is just around the corner. *You* have the power to spread it and help heal this world.

"Hey, Kimberly, I helped feed the homeless once. It made me feel so good and happy about my own life. It's kinda like that bumper sticker, 'Commit Random Acts of Kindness.' Try doing it; it's the best feeling in the world!"

I have read about, talked to, and experienced people who live their lives from this place, a place of miracles, a place of love. Life can be crummy—sometimes, in fact, in can be a real pain in the... When it is this way, all we have to do is ask for a miracle. I have a friend who was ready to divorce his wife, until he listened to a beautiful set of tapes, titled "Return to Love." They are based on the power of love, true love. He listened to the tapes over and over again. When he really listened, and he began to understand what love was, and the power of it in his own life and in his marriage, drastic changes happened. He simply asked for a miracle, and he got one. He is committed to his marriage now, but more importantly, he is committed to love.

"Kimberly, I think many of the readers may be thinking, 'What is this love stuff?' Do you want people going around hugging and kissing everyone and telling them, 'I love you'?"

Well, sometimes that is appropriate and even comfortable; however, I don't think New York City is ready for that, or your neighborhood, for that matter. So, hold on and stick with me. You want miracles to happen, right? Well, you have to listen to the guidelines here and you *must* put them into practice. *Promise me you will try this one. Come on, Promise, promise, promise. Promise! Promise! Promise! Promise! Promise! Promise! Promise!* OK, read on.

Love reminds me of a meadow of beautiful flowers in bloom. With the proper nourishment (water, sunshine and good soil) the flowers will flourish. I've even had plants that were on the verge of dying. After I fed them and gave them nourishment and love, they came back to life. They were even better than ever. Love has that same power with people. If you send out love—genuine love—to other people, they, too, will bloom. You can help change people's lives with the power of your love! *You can do it!*

I have seen people cured of terminal illnesses, reform drug addicts, change hateful people, cure autism and transform millions of people lives—simply by the power of love. You can help transform the world (*Yes, you!*) by learning how to love yourself first, then sharing that love with others. You have power beyond your wildest dreams, so test it and see how much power you have. The greatest self-esteem boost is giving your love away. When you do something special for someone else, without asking or expecting anything in return, the result is self-esteem and fulfillment. All right already, I'll give you some powerful examples.

My girlfriend, Sue, had a niece who was abused in her home. She almost joined a gang, and she used to sneak out through her window and get into all sorts of trouble. She even contemplated murdering someone once. Sue simply loved her

niece, unconditionally. She made her feel safe. She had to spend a lot of time with her, and she listened a lot. She never hit her, like her mother did, she just reasoned her to death. Sometimes, I think she would have preferred the hitting to Sue's looooooong loving lectures. Being hit was familiar to her, it took a while for her to believe in real love and trust it.

The bottom line is that Sue's love transformed this flunking, rebellious teenager. Her niece learned to trust Sue. She only lived with Sue for approximately one year, but she learned about love. Sue also gave a lot of love and help to her parents, so they would be better, more loving parents for their children. Sue's niece is an honor student and gets along with her parents really well now. She hasn't been in any trouble. She has learned about love...they all have.

All it took to transform her life was the love from one person, her Aunt Sue. You can help transform and change even a seemingly impossible, grim, painful, and hopeless life with your love.

I wonder if you are asking yourself, "What on earth does this have to do with the mind and learning?" Hey, that's a good question if it has crossed your mind. The mind is no good without the heart. It is all interrelated. How can we ever be happy if we are just geniuses with no love? **EmpowerMind** is about finding an integration of mind, heart and spirit (the body's important too, but that's a whole other book). Have you seen the movie, *Little Man Tate*? If you have, then you know what I'm talking about. Go rent it if you haven't seen it. It is a great example of the miracle of love. The genius boy in the movie wasn't complete with just being smart. It was equally important for him to be loved. He needed to be mentally challenged, but without the incredible love from his mother, his life would have been...Think about it...*one big Zeeero!*

How Does Love Help Your Learning?

Think about how you learn when you love something. It becomes easy, right? You are sending positive vibes to the brain the subconscious brain cells are saying, "Let's go guys! I can do this, and I can do it well." When you love something or someone, you are automatically in your alpha state. If you are in your alpha state, you can tap into your subconscious, become relaxed and be positive about the sport, subject, event, or person you are involved with at the moment. So, if you start to *love* math and *love* studying it, and feel this love, your relationship with math will change. You will be open to receiving the information. So, tell yourself positive things about math and that you love it. Or, tell yourself you love another tough subject, or just that you love school in general. Remember, your subconscious cannot tell the difference between imagination and reality, so get to it! Love those subjects you used to hate.

Now it's your turn. Let's put some of this into practice. First, for starters, I want you to go out and spread love today, right now! How? Start by loving the room you are in. Set down this book a minute and look around you. Love the place your sitting in. It doesn't matter if you are in a smelly old shack...*just love it!* (Nike's new slogan.) Well, just do it! Do not start reading on until you have done this. It's important that you just...do it!

Love the clothes you're wearing (I'm assuming that you are wearing them now). Love yourself. Give yourself a big hug for reading this book and say out loud, "I really do love you!"

"Hey, loosen up, dudes! It's time for the Hacker Dude opinion. You've learned to make funny faces and sing in the car, for gosh sakes, so this should be a breeze! Come on! Nobody's looking. Just do it!"

See, that wasn't so hard. You think this is nuts? Well, how did you feel after doing that? Did you feel depressed or did you feel a little better? Did your mood change at all? Well, that is your answer! This is the starting block. Now, go love everything for an entire day. I mean *Loooove* that alarm clock in the morning. *Looove* that shower (no matter how bad the pressure is.) Love those people on the bus and in other cars. Love your teachers and bosses. Love your assignments (even math) and the books you read. *Looove* your lunch. Just send out looooove to everything and everyone. You do not, *do not, do not,* have to touch anyone, say "I love you," or even verbally hint at it. You just need to feel it. Practice feeling it. When the worst, I mean like the worst teacher, boss or peer puts you right over the edge, just send him or her a smile filled with real love. What will happen...well, did you see *The Karate Kid*? You will be the winner, and the miracles will begin to happen. So, stop reading right now! Do not continue until you have done this. Go love *everything* for a day. I said *stop* reading *now!* You can read on, but only after you have tried this out. I want you to see if it works, then you can move on to the next advanced level. *Stop!Stop!Stop!Stop!Stop!*

Well, I hope you loved everything for a day before you read on. You still have time. Stop, if you haven't already, go do it and come back.

Sooooooo, what happened? I bet you noticed some changes? If you didn't see them in other people (yet) what changes did you see in yourself? (Write them in.)

_____

_____

_____

Give yourself a pat on the back, I'm really proud of you. Now, every time you think this doesn't work, you can come back to this page and read what you wrote. This will remind you of the miracle of love. It has to start with you. You have to reward yourself mentally ("Hey, way to go! I did it! I tried! I did my best! I went further this time!") in order to start feeling it inside. Love has to be felt by you (you have to love yourself) first, then the love can go out to others.

Next, let's go another step further. (*You can do it!*) This is a real challenge, but I know you are up for it. Try this assignment with people you truly dislike. The more sickening and unworthy you think the person is of your love, the better. You see, then you will truly see if this works. If it seems impossible to love this person, because nobody does, try the magical word *compassion*. Use your imagination (I know you can do that), and imagine why this person is so tough or mean or alone. Maybe this person is scared to have friends, because friends have always hurt him or her in the past. Maybe this person had very mean and cruel parents growing up and learned about pain at an early age. Maybe this person is reaching out for just one person, like you, to not give up on him or her. You could be the one person who makes the difference in this person's life. Are you up for this challenge? Try it, because it is then that you will see miracles. If you still don't believe me, rent the video, *It's a Wonderful Life.* It is a movie showing the power just one person's life has in this world. Your life is just as powerful.

I was following up with Donna, a student at San Rafael High School in California. I told her if she was to do anything that I taught from the course, she should do this. I said forget everything else if you want, and just try this for awhile. I had a specific teacher in mind. Donna said, "Yeah, maybe I'll try it, but not with that teacher! *Anyone but her!*"

I said, "What did you expect me to give you as an assignment—your best friend to try this on?"

Donna didn't respond. I told her, "If you try it on this woman, my bet is that a miracle will happen." She didn't believe me. She thought I was nuts, because she was sure that nothing could help the situation with this teacher. She was a tough one, but finally she agreed. I said, "Hey, this way, you can come back and tell me it didn't work." She left with a commitment to try, but she still thought I was nuts.

Two weeks later, Donna came back for a follow-up session with an amazed look on her face. "You wouldn't believe what happened!" she said. "I sent that 'love energy' thing you told me to do to that teacher, and you won't believe what happened!"

Of course, I was eager and asked, "What?!"

She said, "Well, one day she asked me to stay after class. I'm thinking, *Uh-oh, I'm in trouble now*. I just knew I had done something to make her mad. The teacher said, 'I just wanted to tell you, you look pretty today, and I like your blouse.' " (Mind you, this is a teacher who hasn't even related to the kids as human beings all year.) Donna said she was shocked. This comment, for this teacher, was amazing; Donna experienced a miracle. She only sent her love for two weeks. She was only sending positive thoughts to this teacher. It was only feeling compassion for this teacher, that created this miracle. Imagine the power love really has, *Imagine the power you have!*

I have another embarrassing story to share. It's for sure now, the universe definitely has a sense of humor! In 1989, I was exploring the power of love by reading a book called *How Can I Help*, by Ram Dass. He was talking about really loving people in the present moment and giving to the world by simply doing that. I was committed! I thought there is no time like the present, so I began immediately.

I was on a San Fransisco Muni Bus at the time. I thought, "The next person that sits next to me is going to get love like they have never had before!" Then, I had my chance. A homeless woman boarded and sat next to me. I could smell her alcoholic breath...Basically, I could smell...her. I thought, what a great opportunity. Boy, did I love her. I smiled at her and sent her love like you wouldn't believe. I knew this would change her immediately, because after all, I "followed the directions." Well, she didn't seem to feel a thing; in fact, it appeared that she passed...out. I shut the book and realized maybe there's more to love than just smiling and sending it, and maybe it takes more than just one attempt. It doesn't always happen the first time or the way you expect it to happen. In fact, the only time I have seen love poured out to a person with no response is when the person is under the influence of a drug (this includes alcohol). It doesn't mean it can't work in those cases, too. Just never give up trying! You will know, after some time, if you can reach the person you are sending your love to.

Go out in the world, now, and see what power you have. Go out and love someone! You need to practice. As you can see, with some people, you need to practice over and over again until they receive it. Whatever you do, do not give up. Many of my students, like Donna, haven't given up, and it has changed their lives.

Now, for another secret. This is a biggie. This secret will help you get further ahead in school with no effort. This secret is about teachers. This will show you how to change a B+ to an A, or a failing to a passing grade. Are you ready for the three magical words? OK, here goes, *teachers are humans!* They have houses, families, feelings, hopes, fears and some of them even date. Believe it or not, they don't live to grade your tests in their free time. I know how you're feeling. It was hard for me to believe when I first heard it (a million years ago, when I was in school), but it's true. I always thought they were special, just not like you and me.

So, how does this secret help you? Well, first, if you send love energy to a teacher, the teacher will naturally respond. A thirteen year old, Britney, told me she really "hated" her teacher before she ever "loved" her. Once she started "loving" her, the teacher's whole attitude changed (and so did Britney's). The teacher was so amazed in the shift in Britney, that she decided to take the **EmpowerMind** course to find out what happened. Britney simply loved her, which resulted in love back. I know, you're thinking this would work with anyone but

the teacher you can think of now, but you're wrong! Try it and prove me wrong. Help me on this one, Hacker!

"This totally worked for me in science class. I really sent love to my teacher. She suggested I do some extra credit to help my grade, and she didn't even offer extra credit to the rest of the class. I did it and got a B, when otherwise I would have gotten a C-. I say, Go for it!"

This next one is my favorite example. I have a student, Eric, who had to do a paper for English class on a business person in the community. I was honored that he chose me. I thought he did an excellent job and he is, of course, an advanced **EmpowerMind** student. So, I said, "Why don't we put the **EmpowerMind** philosophy to work here, and prove to you that teachers are human. I'll write a letter to your teacher telling how great you are and how hard you have been working on this paper (which was all true, of course), and you will not only get an A, but we may see a miracle." He was excited, but had no idea what to expect. (Neither did I, but I seldom do.) Of course, part of the deal was that he acted like he didn't know what the letter said, when he handed her the envelope. (It would have been too embarrassing. He just wanted to give it to her and leave the room.) She not only read it, with such pride, to the class, but the whole class applauded him. She's even putting it in his college transcript file. Teachers are human and this one was human in the most beautiful way for Eric. Eric was a bit embarrassed, but what a send-off for the last day of school! He'll never forget it, or her. She was a real gift to him. He might have never known, if he hadn't sent her love. So, go for it! Send love to your teachers *now!*

Now, here's how it helps you with grades and no effort. I have researched this (by asking every teacher I have ever had the privilege of working with) to assure you my answer would be true. If a teacher is figuring out your grade on a test or for your report card, and your grade is between a B+ and an A-, what do you think your teachers would give you? Let's say you're between passing and failing (actually you have failed by five percentage points) what do you think your teachers would give you? If your answers are a "B+" and a "failed grade," it's because you haven't been using this love technique.

All the teachers I asked told me that if they felt that the students had tried, cared (essentially sent positive vibrations L-O-V-E), or had strong feelings about getting a good grade and had expressed them, they would give them the A- and the passing grade. *This was 100%, guys and girls! So wake up! They are human after*

WHAT GOES UP.....   MUST COME DOWN

all! yeah! Simply send love energy to your teachers and to the subject you are studying. (Remember, you have to try and really feel it.) Talk with your teachers about how important it is to do well in their class, and it will help! This takes *no* extra time or energy—just a desire to try it.

Hey, sometimes loving someone doesn't work the first time you do it. Sometimes, people need more. Find yourself a challenge and go for it! Parents, sisters and brothers and teachers are great starters. Go out and love them! See what happens. If it doesn't work with any of them, it will be a surprise. The only times I have seen it not work is when the person you are targeting, is either mentally sick or has drug problems. Often, even in the worst cases, it works anyway. Only you can decide if you have put out all the effort possible. If you can honestly say to yourself, "I have done all I can," then you simply need to "let go." Please write me and let me know your successes, and just try to prove to me it doesn't work. I've never heard of a case yet (from any of my students) that hasn't worked. Is that challenge enough? Now, go out and…(what do you think I'm going to say?) *Just do it!* "Simply"…love.

Summary

To truly be happy in your life and create miracles daily, you must live from a place of love. Love is the key ingredient to true happiness and fulfillment. Without love, life means nothing. Love is the most powerful emotion of all! When you give love, you will automatically get it back. It may not be from the person you just gave it to, but you will always get it back somehow…some day. Love opens a person up in ways that were never possible before. Love makes learning, building relationships and just plain living magical. Hmm…no wonder it is so powerful.

Questions

1. True or False? There are only two kinds of emotions. _____

2. _____ is the most powerful negative emotion and _____ is the most powerful emotion of all.

3. True or False? It is more powerful to forgive than to get revenge. _____

4. Life - Love = _____

5. How can you get more love in your life?
   A. Be open to it.
   B. Tell people you deserve it.
   C. Make people love you, otherwise they will pay dearly!
   D. Give love

6. The power of love is _____ . It creates miracles.

7. True or False? Loving someone means hugging and touching them. _____

8. True or False? People can cure themselves of terminal illnesses through the power of love. _____

9. What happens when we use love in learning?
   A. It brings us to our alpha state
   B. It gets us interested in the subjects or events
   C. Both A and B
   D. None of the above

10. What does it mean to love everything for a day?

    _____

    _____

11. When you give love, you will eventually _____ love.

12. When it is really tough to love someone, you can use your imagination to help you find _____ in your heart.

13. True or False? It's best to practice loving someone you already like. That experience will show if loving someone really makes a difference. _____

14. You can change the world, by the power of your _____ .

15. World's greatest secret: Teachers really are _____ after all.

Dear loving student/reader,

    I wish I could be sharing this chapter of love with you in person. This chapter is my favorite because it is written from my heart to yours. I wish I could look into your loving eyes and wash away all your pain, worries and fear. But since I cannot be with you physically, I would like you to feel my presence spiritually. Close your eyes and imagine me giving you a huge warm loving hug. You deserve it for just being wonderful you. Also you have earned it by truly living this chapter. Know that you are in my thoughts and prayers.

I hear and I forget
I see and I remember
I do and I understand
— *Chinese proverb*

When a child is born, only one goal is given. That single goal is to live an extraordinary life.

Every human is given great potential when he or she is born.

Each human on earth is given the ability to have an exceptional life by having extraordinary experiences. Experience is the best knowledge there is...

For one to succeed with this single goal in life, one must have the equipment to do it. Every human is given a special gift; their unique and individualized equipment.

Be aware that your individual gifts create your individuality.

First discover them.

Then learn how to express them.

With self-discovery and inner growth, you can learn to be your own best friend. You will be your own companion throughout life. Be kind to your friend. That friendship will always be there for you.

Instincts. Your natural inclinations. You have them even now. Develop them continuously. Experiences and knowledge help you "build them up" like exercise builds muscles. Experiences most definitely add to the capability of your instincts. View life like a tourist would see it. Look at things every day as if you are seeing them for the first time. Be curious. Be creative. Learn to do things a different way than other people, learn your own way of doing things, learn to love learning. Learn to ask questions. Learn to expand your creativity, self awareness, persistence, enthusiasm and positive attitude. Travel! This all creates extraordinary lives!

Peter Earley
From *Do You Have A Mentor Yet?*

Chapter Nine

Create and Materialize Your Goals and Dreams

Overview

The Vision is referred to as "The Big Picture" in the EmpowerMind course. In this chapter, we will be taking "The Big Picture" a step further toward "The Vision." This will explain to you how to create and materialize visions you have for yourself. Does wealth sound good? How about happiness, love, and all the chocolate ice cream you can eat? If this sounds "appetizing" to you, then read on, because this chapter offers a guideline, a map of how to create and materialize your dreams.

Questions

1. Our subconscious cannot tell the difference between _____ and _____ .

2. The following four ingredients are essential for success. Put them in the correct order.
   A. Surrender and trust
   B. Look at the details to your goal
   C. Make sure your basic vision is made out of love
   D. Set intermittent goals to create your vision

3. How long does it take to make or break a habit? _____

4. True or False? We can accomplish only things that we believe we can accomplish. _____

5. Everyone has:
   A. An inner genius
   B. A strong left brain
   C. Strong whole brain learning

    D. A desire to be great

    E. All of the above

6. Like in the movie *Hook*, you need to realize your_____ can create anything!

7. True or False? "The Vision" is just about the same as "The Big Picture," only it refers more to life rather than school. _____

8. What does getting a "yes" answer mean in accomplishing what we want in our lives?

    Great! You decided to read on, this means we already have something in common. We both want to create more fulfilling lives. We are willing to continue learning *and* we both have our...dreams.

    What is the vision?

    The main step in the vision is asking yourself, "What outcome do I want to see for myself?" What is the big picture? So often, we get so obsessed with details, which are unimportant in producing the end result, that we lose sight of the goal, the big picture, the vision.

    If you could see the end result, what would it be? See it! Visualize it! Look at where you are going, before you attempt to get there. Isn't it easier to look at a map or a set of directions and get an idea of where you are going, instead of following each bit of information at a time? You see, if you know where you are supposed to arrive, you may figure out a short-cut or may remember the construction signs along one route. It's the same way in life. We want to look for short cuts, easier paths and all paths and roads with as little construction and obstruction as possible, that still take us where we want to go. Some people have chosen the wrong short-cuts, and it has led to pain and suffering. It's true that all journeys toward

success have unexpected detours. It's up to you to look ahead, while still paying attention to the road in front of you, so you can stay on course.

"Before I understood 'the vision' and how it all worked, I fell in a lot of sewers along my path. My life is on a much happier road now."

With the vision, you won't even notice the detours even when you are on them. These detours will just become part of the process that will eventually help you realize your vision.

Something that I have found useful in my life when making a decision (a big decision), is to simply relax or meditate and imagine myself at my deathbed. I'm 100 years old (I'm sure I won't die that soon!). I am looking back on my life and the decisions I've made. I reflect on my choices. The specific choices are the ones I am about to make in my life now. I see two doors in front of me. I choose the first door and see how life turned out by actually experiencing (in my mind) that decision. Then I choose the other door and reflect back to see how the other decision turned out. Simply, this method can give you some perspective. All of a sudden, flunking a test or missing a date doesn't seem like such a big deal. Just try it. It may or may not work for you, but it is definitely worth trying.

It is also very important to *simplify, simplify, simplify*.

Suppose—and it shouldn't be much of a stretch to imagine this—you have an overwhelming work load at school and some tough teachers. Practice these first two steps:

Step 1. Ask yourself, What is the big picture of this situation? (The big picture is the desired outcome, so ask yourself that first.) You may answer, "I want to get all A's and B's and have my weekends free to play around." Simplify more! "I want a B+ average and two days of free time per week." You only simplify more if it works for you, and still helps you reach your overall desired outcome.

Step 2. Next, you need to look at all the options. Here are just a few. (See if you can see any others.) Look at the teachers who are easy, the courses that are easy, and where you will have to spend most of your time. Make a real effort to receive A's or B's in all the easy subjects, then, it will offset your difficult classes and you'll put in less study time. (What on earth does that mean?) When you put your first efforts on the courses that are easiest and come most naturally to you (and your overall goal is a specific G.P.A.), then you will get the A's and B's in the easier courses, with less time and effort. This will automatically bring up your overall G.P.A. in less time and with less effort. If you have tough teachers, send them tons of love energy (which you should be doing with all your teachers, by the way). Can you get extra credit in any of the courses? Maybe the extra credit is easy for you. Should you drop a class or move down to a class that isn't so advanced? (Do this only if you don't really need the class for anything in your future.) Study with partners? Use the appropriate **EmpowerMind** study tools where needed. The list seems limitless.

Are you thoroughly confused, yet? Well, let's try another example.

"And confuse them more, Kimberly? Just kidding!"

Well, I hope this example will clarify what I mean.

This example is from real life. When I worked for Pepsi-Cola, I was supposed to sell, and have my driver deliver, as many cases as possible with the least amount of overtime.

Big Picture: Sell and deliver as many cases as possible, with the least amount of overtime.

I was given no prizes or money to build the driver's incentive. They just told me he was lucky to have a job. Well, I looked at all my options and thought about them. I knew my desired outcome (my bosses took care of that for me), but I didn't know how to get my driver motivated.

Now, I thought about my "options."

1. I knew I was given no incentives from the company to motivate my driver.

2. I brain-stormed with myself. I figured, I better find out what motivated my driver. So, I thought about it from my driver's perspective. I wanted to see what *his* "desired outcome" was. His wife just had a baby. I found out he wanted more time off. So I asked him if he would appreciate it if I set a quota of a certain number of cases he had to deliver per week, instead of per day. Then, if he finished in two hours or ten hours, I'd still pay him for the whole day, but he would not get paid for overtime, unless we talked about it first.

He not only loved the idea, but he was the top performing driver in the state, with the least amount of overtime. But, most importantly, he was happy and so was I!

I don't know if you have picked this up yet, but the reason we are figuring out these examples is to teach you to work less, play more and be happy. You see, learning how to create visions in your life is kind of like sky-diving. If you get 99% correct on the test, but simply forget to pull the chord, then…you die. If you get all A's, but you are miserable, then…your happiness dies. Keeping your visions alive and your priorities clear, creates happiness. Wouldn't you rather spend a little time thinking now than more time making mistakes, wasting time, studying and being unhappy? Oh, good, then I'll continue.

Are you ready for a challenging example? (Hey, where's your positive attitude?) OK, just to make sure you have or will arrive at an understanding of the vision I'm referring to, I will paint a picture for you. (By the way, Hacker helped me with this one.) Let's assume the following:

1. You are a high school student; if you can raise $500 in the summer (it's May now) your parent(s) will let you go on a student cruise to the Bahamas.

2. You have two younger brothers, ages 12 and 13.

3. You have an opportunity to choose three jobs:

   Paper route ($40/week, $480/summer) 4:30 a.m.-6:00 a.m.

   Mowing lawns (no guarantee on how many lawns you would mow) you estimate 2/week or $40/week, $480/summer.

   Baby sitting your neighbors, three screaming brats four days/week (Monday-Thursday) from 9:00-5:00 p.m. for $125/week, $1,500/summer.

4. You want to play tennis in a league every Tuesday and Thursday from 5:00-7:00, so you can make varsity next year; it's your favorite sport.

5. Let's fantasize here. Your mom says she'll be home from 3:00 p.m. until the next morning, everyday, and will help support you however she can.

6. If you make the money early, you can spend the last two weeks of summer with your buddies at their cabin on the lake. There are sailboats, motorboats, skiing, tubing, etc. Plus, there are lots of cool kids on the lake.

Don't panic! This is not, I repeat, this is not a math horror. Let go of those ugly tapes in your head. This is simply about life's choices. Re-read the six assumptions, *now*!

Thank you!

Let's look deeper and add some more steps to "simplify."

Before making your decisions, read the following "steps to the vision":

1. When making this decision, you must look at your desired outcome of the situation: the overall vision, the big picture. Stop here and *think about it*. Ask yourself questions like: What are my options? Will I be happy I did this a year from now? Twenty years from now? Will this make my overall school career better, or my overall life better? And for the biggie, will this make me happy? *Simplify, simplify, simplify!*

2. Then, ask yourself the following:

   A. What are the next most important options to consider?

   B. What details, if any, are needed to support my decision?

   C. If there are obstacles, how can I overcome them in choosing the appropriate course of action?

   D. If there were obstacles in question "C," will I be able to eliminate these obstacles and how?" (Be careful not to limit your options and ideas.)

Now, write down your answers to the above questions. Remember, there are no right answers—only you can decide what is right for you.

1A. What are my options? _____

_____

_____

_____

1B. Will I be happy I did this in a year from now? _____

1C. Will I be happy I did this twenty years from now? _____

1D. Will this make my overall school career or life better? _____

1E. Will this make me happy? _____

2A. What are the most important options to consider? _____

_____

_____

2B. What details, if any, are needed to support my decision? _____

_____

_____

_____

_____

2C. If there are any obstacles, how can I overcome them? _____

_____

_____

_____

2D. If there were obstacles in "C," will I be able to eliminate these obstacles and, if so, how? _____

_____

_____

_____

_____

3. You may have your answers already, but if you don't, *relax!* Let your subconscious take over and help you with this choice.

4. Once you have made your decision, see yourself accomplishing it successfully. (Yes! Shut your eyes, sit back and enjoy your vision. This is a good time to listen to the "Goals" side of your tape and visualize your success.)

5. Surrender! Let go of all fears, tension and control, because you know you made the right decisions. Even if your decisions weren't "perfect," you probably had a much happier ending, than if you tried accomplishing all of this the "UNEmpowerMind" way.

Now, did you really look at the big picture, your overall vision? Did you limit yourself or did you look at all the possibilities? Think about it! Hey, don't read on yet...think about it, even re-read it. Was there anything you overlooked? (How's that for a simple question? "Not!") Write your overall vision. What is it that you want?

_____

_____

_____

Now, let's look at the possibilities together. Yeah, just you and me. It's kind of like a puzzle. If your big picture is deciding you want it all, then we know the following: You need $500 by the end of summer. You need to get off work by at least, 4:45 p.m. on Tuesdays and Thursdays (so you can make it to tennis by 5:00). You need to be done at least two weeks before the end of summer (so you can go to the cabin on the lake).

Let's set this up so we can see it better...*simplify, simplify, simplify!*

Needs (the big picture):

  1. $500

  2. 4:45 Tues./Thurs.

  3. Done two weeks before summer's over

That wasn't too hard was it? Aren't the needs fairly obvious? Now, let's look at our big picture options. They are the following:

Work the paper route, $480/summer (4:30-6:00 a.m.).

Mow lawns estimated $480/summer.

Baby sit four days/week $1,500 (9:00 a.m.-5:00 p.m.).

OK, what do we do now? *Simplify, simplify, simplify!*

Options (the big picture):

  1. Paper route 4-6 a.m. ($480)

  2. Mow lawns (two lawns/week estimated $480)

  3. Baby sit (9-5 p.m. four days/week $1,500)

Now, when we write options, does this mean it's one or the other? Does this mean we have no control? Does this mean we are powerless to change these choices around to make a win-win situation? I think not! You, however, should think: is it as simple as these three options, just the way they are? Is it one or the other?

Think about this before you read on.

What really are your options? Look at them! Be creative, for gosh sakes. You are smart and you can figure out that there are always more options than there simply appear to be.

Can you combine some of these options? If your answer is yes, how would it work out? Are you totally confused yet? Well, let's see what some of the other options are. So far we have three simple options. Now let's go for three more.

Option number 4: Work the paper route and mow the lawns. (Seven and a half hours on paper route and two lawns/week equals $480 x 2 = $960 (well over the $500, plus tons of free time. You could even take off the last two weeks and still make over $500.)

Option number 5: Just baby sit, make $1,250 (because you take off the last two weeks for the lake). Skip tennis. You still have three days off a week and an extra $750 to buy whatever you want. You could also hire someone to give you private tennis lessons, and you would have a lot of extra time to play. You may not even need to work next summer.

Option number 6: This is the last option we will look at reviewing. (I confess, this is *my* favorite.) Let's first look at the details a bit more. Have you forgotten you have two brothers with nothing to do but play all summer (and who idolize you, of course). You have a willing mother who verbally volunteered her services from 3:00 p.m. until bedtime to help you.

Hacker, tell the readers what you think.

"You have support oozing out all over the place and you don't even know it yet."

But, you will...

Have you even looked at these "details" yet? So, what can you do? How can they help you reach your optimal goal with the least amount of your effort? Shut your eyes and think about it.

Option number 6: I say do all of them!

You can do your paper route until 6:00 a.m., then come home and rest if you need to until 8:45 a.m. Then you can baby sit from 9:00-5:00 four days a week. You may even get your brothers to volunteer help. Your mom takes over from 4:30-5:00 on Tuesdays and Thursdays so you can play tennis. You get the mowing jobs for your brothers, and you pay them half. They mow once a week and are happy. You just check up on their mowing quickly, to see that is done properly. In six weeks, you'll make $1,010 (route $240, mowing $120, babysitting $750).

You'll get half the summer off, you'll have made double the money you need, and you can still play tennis and get three days off a week. Whew! Not bad, eh? Life can and will turn out this way, if you follow the steps to the vision.

There were several additional choices to the example I gave you. There are *no* right or wrong answers. You are in the driver's seat of life. Do you see now that maybe there are more choices than you ever imagined? When you are trying to make a decision or you have a problem in your life, use the "steps to the vision" to help yourself. Learn to look at *all* your options and all the details. Get help from others and simplify!

Here's a great example a student of mine used. Her name is Angel, and she is thirteen years old. She had a book report due, among many other assignments. She knew she couldn't adequately spend time to complete it. So, she used the big picture approach instead of the option (as she saw it) of receiving a failing grade for not writing the report. She saw that the book had a book cover that recaptured the whole story, so she read that and then quickly breezed through reading the book. She did not reread the book at all. She did her report in about a half an hour from the book "cover" and her quick reading of the book. She got an A on the report and was able to spend her time on her other subjects. She also used another report she did on a famous person, that she typed for extra credit in her computer class. She used her mind and her creative genius, instead of receiving what appeared to be a failing grade. Using the big picture method doesn't have to be complicated. In fact, it's the opposite. Make it easy!

Part II: Steps to the Vision

If you cannot see a desired outcome, it will not happen; this is a guarantee. We cannot create in our lives something that our subconscious cannot see, feel or accept. I know a man who could never see himself out of debt, working in a job he loved, and living his dream. Guess what? He's been in debt for twenty years, has a job he hates and would have continued on this program, except he "visualized" a different "big picture." Now, he's on his way to living his dream. You must be open to life's possibilities and choices. When you are closed to new paths by your old programming, by your limited association base, you lose sight of what is really important. You will lose sight of what will bring you success and ultimately make you happy.

Think about what you would like to create for yourself in your life? Now, take a minute, shut your eyes and visualize it. Shut your eyes! *You can do it!*

Did you see visions for yourself? Powerful, huh?

What sources can assist you in order to provide the support you need? Think about some options.

Remember, you must take one step at a time. You see, only you can create the vision for yourself to make it successful. Often others will try to create a vision for you. The problem is that the vision is theirs not yours. It's good to get input from people you respect, then evaluate it. Ultimately, you need to make your own choice. As taught in the course, when reading the chapters in a book, you must look at where you are going in order to understand the process along the way. The overall vision is void of specifics, details and control. It is just getting in touch with what you want to create in your life.

This overall vision must lead to the last step, "Surrender." Here's an example of what can happen when we start with step one, of "The Vision," and complete the last step, "Surrender."

A friend of mine, Kathrine, got in a car accident several years ago. Her daughter was severely injured and was in a coma for several weeks. Kathrine stayed with her every day, holding her hand, dreaming of their lives together as a happy family again. She tortured herself with worry. She just knew her daughter had to pull out of it. She was sending her love and pleading with her to come back to her. Finally, after the doctors advised her to get some rest, and she felt powerless, she surrendered. She stopped trying to control the unknown.

Kathrine knew she had done all she could. It was time to let go and surrender to a higher force. When she finally did, her daughter regained consciousness and slowly moved on to a full recovery. This woman, my dear friend, learned how to surrender even in the most difficult of circumstances.

Sometimes things are outside of our "control." We can do our best and put our whole heart and soul into something and it still may not work out according to our plan. Believe it or not, we don't always know what is best for us. Often we can look back and realize that everything did have a purpose, a reason, a lesson. Our greatest lesson is probably surrender, because we have to believe we have done our best, let go of control and surrender to whatever the outcome may be. We have to trust that things will work out for the best. Think in your life when you were positive that something was going to turn out, or should turn out, a certain way and it didn't. Now that you look back, did it turn out for the best in the long run? Your answer is most likely going to be "yes." Next time you still want to control, after you have done all you can, think about a time when you just "let go" and it all turned out for the best.

When we control our lives too much we can miss wonderful opportunities and blessings along the way. This is when you only see the destination on your journey, without being in the moment and checking out the scenery along the way. Our minds are powerful, and they can attract something into our lives if we program them enough. But what if we are wrong?

I had a tutoring session with a man one day. He told me that if he "let go" and "surrendered," he would never attract the job he was trying to obtain with a specific company. He was brilliant, and I knew he could do anything he put his mind to achieving. This included attracting the perfect job. My concern was, what if he took this job with the "specific" company and got involved in a contract, then lost an opportunity to find the "perfect job" because he was stuck in a contract?

There's a fine line here. You end up "controlling" when the universe is giving you "No" answers, and you struggle to try to make it work anyway. Surrender is about listening to the messages the universe gives you. Control is about ignoring those messages and pushing (I mean pushing) forward anyway. You can only do so much, then sometimes you must simply (there's that word again) surrender.

If Abraham Lincoln hadn't had so many failures (failed marriage, eight political defeats, nervous breakdown, etc.) he probably wouldn't have been the great compassionate President that he was. He always put out his best. But, if he had surrendered more, he could have avoided some of his heartache. He pushed and pushed and pushed. He still became President, but at what expense to himself? His happiness, and eventually, his life.

There is no such thing as failure, unless you put a time limit on your goals. Think about that. You have the rest of your life to accomplish great things, no

matter how old you are. Colonel Sanders started his chicken business when he was in his 60's.

It's not that you should overlook the details on your way to your goal, but you must concentrate on them at the appropriate time. It's when you have given the situation your best effort and followed all of the steps, that you must let go and know you have done all you can. If you still try to control the outcome after this point, it can be damaging to you. It took a great deal of heartache until my friend, Kathrine, learned the lessons of trust and surrender. I hope that you will be able to minimize your mistakes by following a simple formula. This formula will open doors for you and miracles will begin to happen in your life.

There are four key ingredients in this formula for making a vision success-ful—once you have seen the Overview, the result of that vision. This is a simplified version, yet also an advanced level of the formula you read about earlier in this chapter, "Steps to the vision."

The Four Basic Steps

1. The basis of all your visions must be made out of love.
2. You should have some intermittent goals in the vision.
3. You should then look at the details of the goals and rate those details in order of importance to the whole vision.
4. Lastly, you must surrender the outcome of your vision to the universe. Then you must trust. Live as though your outcome to the vision has already happened. Remember, your subconscious mind does not know the difference between imagination and reality.

Now, I will discuss each step of "*The Four Basic Steps*" in detail and each will be followed with examples and stories about how it all works.

In the first step, you will look at the intent of your vision. Is this vision for your higher good? Is it for the world's higher good? *Is this vision based on love?* Love is a cosmic phenomenon; it draws in gifts of abundance. Abundance is not always in the material realm. In fact, most often it is not. Think of the most memorable or moving experiences in your life. Were these memorable experiences surrounded by money and material goods, or simply by love?

If you can honestly say love is the basis of your vision, then you are on the right track. Let's do a little experiment. Are you with me? Good! I think you're going to enjoy this one. Think about one thing you would like to happen for yourself this year. See the big picture—the end result. Shut your eyes and really visualize this.

We all have to start somewhere. You can even do this with your "Goals" tape and visualize it in your alpha state.

Now, ask yourself if this was coming from a place of love and higher good for you or the universe. If you can answer yes, then read on, because you are ready for step two of "The Vision." If it wasn't, then try again, but this time come from a place of love.

Before you move on, would you like an example of how this all works? OK, here we go! You are about to participate in a sport. Choose your sport. Pick any sport, even if you don't currently play one. Remember, your imagination can create anything you want in your life. Now, this time when you shut your eyes, visualize your desired outcome. You are being carried out on shoulders as the hero, the crowd cheering, team winning, etc. Visualize your desired outcome. Remember, all you are practicing is "The Big Picture," not the details on how you got there. Do you see the difference yet? When you get into your loving alpha state (take two deep breaths), shut your eyes and just visualize the end result.

Was this a vision based on love? Is it for your higher good? Or, is it based on greed, ego or revenge? Sometimes, this isn't clear at first. Becoming the best you can be is based on love, love for yourself. If your vision is achieving your best for the whole team, then that is a good start. If it is based on being the hero, gaining more popularity (getting more dates) or getting revenge on an opponent, then it isn't based on love. It should be based on something like doing your best or having the most fun possible. Or, it may simply be playing your best to help the whole team succeed.

Using visualization in the alpha state is often how Olympic athletes perform so well under pressure. Their subconscious has been programmed for their desired result, the big picture; and since the subconscious doesn't know the difference between…(You've got it by now, don't you?) the subconscious cannot accept any other visualized outcome. The steps and details needed to achieve the outcome may vary, but the final result will be the same.

In the second step, you will set up intermittent goals for the vision. Intermittent goals are small steps. Look at it like running up a staircase with 200 steps. If you concentrate on all 200 steps to begin with, it's overwhelming. But, if you concentrate on one step at a time, it becomes much easier. OK, I'll give you a practical example. Let's say you have six classes, you want to be in sports and you want a lot of friends. If you think about having all of that at once it can be overwhelming. But, if you think of one class at a time, one friend at a time and one sport one day at a time, it will seem easier. It all goes back to…*simplify, simplify!* It's the same with goals. Concentrate on one of your goals at a time and visualize the outcome daily. Live as though you have already been blessed with the outcome. These small goals and your visualizing the outcome, on a daily basis, will make achieving your vision much easier.

Remember, the subconscious doesn't know the difference between imagination and reality. Tell them, Hacker, tell them like it is.

"So imagine, just simply imagine! If you saw the movie Hook you will know what I mean by 'imagine.' Think happy thoughts, eat the food that isn't there (yet) and believe. Like the scene in Hook, where Peter Pan made the food appear by use of his imagination, you can create the same things in your life by tapping into your imagination."

We all have the ability, because (one more time) our subconscious cannot tell the difference between...what? Yes! You have got it! Our subconscious cannot tell the difference between imagination and reality. Live your life as though the outcome has already taken place. Yes, it is true. Sometimes you will run into detours, but they may simply be adventures in disguise.

Well, it looks as though it's time for another example. Let's assume you're still visualizing the sporting event. You have already visualized "the big picture." Now, it's time to ask yourself, "What are some intermittent goals I can set to help me achieve this desired outcome?" Maybe these goals are working out, visualizing success for ten minutes everyday, reading up on the sport, etc. You must decide what these goals are for you. Now set these goals inorder of priority. If you could only do one, what would it be? Then, which is the next most important? And so on and so on. Then visualize yourself achieving one goal at a time, while still keeping the vision of the "big picture" in your mind. Remember the 200 steps...you can see the top, but you only focus on one step at a time. You must never lose sight of the top of the staircase, the "big picture." As you visualize each goal you must start actually (this is the fun part), physically accomplishing each goal. This leads us to the next section, under "The details."

In the third step you have already seen the big picture and you are working on one of your goals in order to achieve your desired "big picture." It's time to look even closer at what details need to be taken care of in order to achieve one goal at a time. Details are the specifics that make your goal achievable, which makes your big picture achievable. Without details, you may tend to make mistakes that are easily avoidable.

Let's look at our example with the sporting event. You have seen the overall desired outcome. You've visualized intermittent goals along the way. Now you need to set up the specifics to help you achieve those goals simply and with as little effort as possible. Let's assume your first goal was to work out one hour a day. The details may be: Where? When? How much? What kind of workout? Do I need help? What support do I need? Will I have a ride to and from the workout place? This is where you ask the: *Why? Where? When? How? What? With whom?* questions. These are usually fairly standard for each set of details, regardless of the accomplishment

or goal you want to achieve. So, ask these questions when you come to the detail section of your vision. Without details, you can make a lot of tiresome, needless, critical mistakes. So...get out there and practice!

Next, you're going to look at the most overlooked step of all: *Step 4...Surrender!* This is the step that will propel you beyond everyone else, because this is when you let go of the controlling. What I mean by controlling is the worry, the fear that your desired outcome won't happen "perfectly"—the exact way you want it. You see, you have seen the overall vision, you've set intermittent goals, you have taken care of the details, so there is nothing left for you to do, but trust and believe. This is often the most difficult one for people to understand and practice. If we let it go and surrender to a higher power, to our super-conscious, then we don't have to control or worry because it is out of our hands and we've let go of control. Read on, maybe the next story will help clarify what I mean.

Another friend of mine was in a tight financial situation in her life. She was just in the midst of starting her own business. She knew there were no immediate signs of money coming in to her. She received a packet from a company, called World Weave, promoting a trip to South Africa. It was a spiritual adventure for women. She read it thoroughly, knowing she couldn't afford to go. She listened to her heart and really felt that there was reason she should be on this trip. She saw the vision of herself in South Africa. Then, she saw money coming in to pay for the trip. She wasn't sure how it would happen, but she felt drawn to the trip. The trip promised a lot of spiritual growth for her and her higher good. She figured she should start taking her own advice for a change.

She first surrendered and meditated, asking for signs to support her decision. She just sat with it a few days, then she decided to call the travel/tour company. They said that if she were to go on the February 26 trip, she would receive $1,000 off the trip. Also, this specific trip would be televised by a nationally syndicated TV show (this could prove to be a business opportunity for her). These were two "yes" votes.

Then, she met a woman a few days later who brought a lot of unexpected clients to her business. These clients paid their money for her services just before Christmas, when everyone seems to be out of money. This unexpected business paid for over half the trip. Hmm...you guessed it: "yes" number 3. Oh, by the way, the woman who brought all these people to her business out of nowhere was named "Angel." That was "yes" number 4.

Three weeks later (as she struggled to pay her rent) she received a check in the mail for $500 from her great aunt in Germany. Her aunt just said that she wanted her to be happy and enjoy it! That's "yes" number 5. It was clear from the first few "yes's" that this was supposed to happen. Listen to your heart and the signs of support will surround you. If you are receiving "no" answers from the universe, there may be something that isn't right about your vision that you may want to change, or you may just be asking at the wrong time. Be patient and be careful about setting too many details at this point. By the way, she met a radio talk show host on the plane who wanted to have her on his show. (Three months later, she was on KFI's talk show, in Los Angeles. She had her greatest response ever and made 90% of the total cost of her trip!)

Surrender!

Some people she met in South Africa were involved in education and wanted her to come back and do work with them. She also gained wonderful friends, including a friendship with the producer of the nationally syndicated TV show. (I know this works, because I don't teach things I haven't experienced and, just maybe, I am my own friend this time. It's about time I learn to practice this! Oh, she also wrote the courses **EmpowerMind #2** and **EmpowerMind #3** on that trip....)

Now, I'm going to really take you a step further. This step is the power of love and how it can help support positive outcomes for people other than yourself. You have the power to help positively change other people's lives. So, wake up, pay attention, and read on.

Another friend of mine, Dan, was telling me how strong his mother was when he grew up. My guess is that she had strong visions of who her children would be and who they were capable of becoming. She wouldn't let anything stand in her way, not even a school system. It sounded like her intentions were out of love and the higher good of her child. Dan was labeled "learning disabled." He needed "special education." This mother believed her son was smart and fought to get him into regular classes. Dan had thought he was stupid, so he figured, "Why should I study? It won't help anyway." You see, his "programming" from his dad, who only finished the sixth grade, was that education "wouldn't help, anyway." Well, his mother's vision was not only strong enough to get him into the regular classes and through high school, but also through his doctorate program and through medical school. He is a neurologist and has a patent on a nerve-growth synthesis for spinal chord injury victims. He said he would have never gone to college if it weren't for his mother fighting for him. The power of his mother's vision was strong. The power of her love was limitless.

Well now, if that wasn't powerful enough, wait until I tell you about Kathy, the great runner. Kathy was a fabulous runner, had even run in a marathon, but then she was in a terrible accident and fell into a coma. The doctors weren't sure if she'd ever be better or even regain consciousness. Kathy's mother stayed with her day and night and filled her room with positive pictures and posters of Kathy's life. She put up a lot of her running pictures. The doctors kept telling her she was crazy to stay with her daughter, and that her daughter would probably never recover. As Kathy's mother sat next to her, holding her hand, tears of hope rolling down her cheeks, she told Kathy over and over again how much she loved her and how terrific she was, and that she would run again. Within a year, Kathy was not only out of her coma, but she ran in a marathon. The power of love *is limitless!*

When you have made it through each of these steps, don't forget to give thanks to yourself for a job well done. You must also give thanks to anyone who assisted you. Most often these are our teachers. Don't ever forget to thank them. We must always be grateful and show humility for our accomplishments, because we could never achieve our successes completely alone. Always remember **"The power of love is limitless."**

Now, I'd like you to incorporate these steps into your life. The fact that you are either in the **EmpowerMind** course or reading this book (or both) shows that you are on the right track, and committed to your own growth. This is a great start and an important first step. I want to support you for starting here.

Write down five things you would like to see for yourself in your life. Imagine you are 40+ years old and describe what you want your life to look like.

1. _____

2. _____

3. _____

4. _____

5. _____

Now, ask yourself what income you will need to support this lifestyle and what type of support you will need from other people or resources to help you achieve your life dream.

_____

_____

_____

What kind of jobs will produce the income you will need?

_____

_____

Now, ask yourself if you will need a college education, a trade-school education, on-the-job experience, etc., to achieve this job position.

_____

_____

Now that you know what you need to do to help get you to this place, think about your life now. What immediate action do you need to take to help prepare yourself for the above step, which will prepare you for the step above that one and so on. If it's college you need to pursue, then you need to get good grades in school. If it's job experience, then get involved. What do you need to do? If you're unsure, ask someone who could help assist you with your answers. Always go to someone whom you respect and trust, and whom you view as successful in the area in which you need help. You should never have role models or mentors who do not live the advice they are teaching you. Talk is cheap. Examples are powerful, inspirational and real! Write your first step of immediate action.

_____

_____

_____

_____

_____

Well, we certainly cannot stop here. You remember what you've been taught about long-term memory. You do remember, don't you? OK, just in case, I'll repeat it. Long-term memory is possible when you become emotionally involved with the material and when you repeat and review information. So, get emotionally involved, re-write the steps of the dreams in your life, and either put them into a relaxation tape (because it takes how long to make or break a habit? Three to five weeks...), or hang them up so you can read your dreams daily. With your dreams reinforced on a daily, or even a weekly basis, your subconscious will create it for you in your life. Why? You already know why.

Now choose the vision that you would like to look at in your life. Follow the four steps for your chosen vision.

Write these four steps out and put them on your mirror or some place you can read them daily. Always remember that you control your life. You have choices. You can always get help for anything. You are a powerful, bright and beautiful human being. You have genius potential. Start visualizing your success! Set your goals! Handle the details (or get someone else to handle them for you)! Surrender and trust! Please share your successes with others so they, too, can reach their genius potential. Remember, whatever you give, you will receive back in greater abundance. And most of all remember the power of what is limitless? *Yes!* You have got it… *"Love!"*

Summary

You have the ability to create what you want in your life. You need to start by following the "four basic steps" outlined in this chapter. It is also important to know that you may need help and support along the way. Choose people wisely, people who have demonstrated success in their lives, to help you succeed. Use visualizations on a daily basis to help support your goals. Believe in yourself, love yourself, and learn to be your own best friend. Give thanks to yourself for your efforts and to those who have supported you along the way.

Questions

1. Our subconscious cannot tell the difference between _____ and _____ .

2. The following four ingredients are essential for success. Put them in the correct order.
   A. Surrender and trust
   B. Look at the details to your goal
   C. Make sure your basic vision is made out of love
   D. Set intermittent goals to create your vision

3. How long does it take to make or break a habit? _____

4. True or False? We can accomplish only what we believe we can accomplish.

   _____

5. Everyone has:
    A. An inner genius
    B. A strong left brain
    C. Strong whole brain learning
    D. A desire to be great
    E. All of the above

6. Like in the movie, "Hook," you need to realize your _____ can create anything!

7. True or False? "The Vision" is just about the same as "the Big Picture," only it refers more to life rather than school. _____

8. What does getting a "yes" answer mean in accomplishing what we want in our lives? _____

9. If you get a "no" answer it probably means:
    A. The "yes" answer is right around the corner
    B. That you are a loser
    C. That the timing isn't right
    D. That you need to clarify your vision better
    E. Both C and D

10. Can you help change other people's lives by the power of love? If so, how?

    _____

    _____

    _____

11. Visions only work for:
    A. Lucky people
    B. People who believe in them and reinforce the vision in their lives
    C. People who act happy all the time
    D. People who go to church or synagogue every week

12. What happens when you get hung up on details?
    A. You can lose sight of the vision.
    B. You will become a left brain person
    C. You will succeed at any cost
    D. You will miss the chocolate chips in the ice cream
    E. A, B and C are correct

13. How do visualizations help athletes succeed? _____

_____

14. True or False? Without details, you may tend to make mistakes that are

easily avoidable. _____

15. What are the six questions you ask in step 3 of the details? (Hint: One of

them is "what?") _____

_____

_____

_____

_____

_____

16. True or False? Long-term memory is formed only by picturing or visualizing

something. Think about it! _____

17. Always give thanks to_____ and

_____ when you have achieved each step toward success.

18. There is no such thing as failure unless you put a _____ on your goals.

19. If you have tried everything you know, with the steps to "The Vision," and

still can't solve your problem then go to _____ .

20. *Extra Credit*: What are you going to say or do when you get discouraged,
    when you have received a few "no" answers, when people aren't supporting

    you the way you want? _____

_____

Chapter Ten

Taking Notes By Doodling and Drawing

Overview

This chapter will take the pain out of note taking. It will be more like doodling. Are you ready to goof off and take good notes at the same time? Looking at the illustrations will explain to you how easy it can really be. Well, read on....

Questions

1. What are the four categories for note taking?

_____

_____

_____

_____

2. Why would I only have three questions for this chapter? _____

_____

_____

3. Write down two different methods of note taking.

_____

_____

This mini-chapter is an example of using "The Big Picture" in learning to take notes. You will use similar basic steps, as you did in "The Vision," but you will apply them to a subject you are taking notes on. Again, these steps are :

    1. The big picture

    2. The subtopics

3. The details

4. Tie it all together/any miscellaneous information

When taking notes, it is best if you can focus on the speaker and listen instead of writing. Hacker knows this.

"This way you can let your imagination go wild and get away with it. It's like you can doodle and not get in trouble for it."

You've got it Hacker!

When taking notes this way, you allow yourself physical freedom so you can become emotionally involved with the subject matter. If you are listening intently, versus writing furiously, you will have a much better chance of getting emotionally involved in the material. Remember what happens when we become emotionally involved? We remember things better!

Do you want to take better notes, but you always lose part of what the lecturer is saying, by concentrating on your lengthy notes? Have you ever asked the person next to you what was just said and missed what the lecturer was currently saying in the process? Well, there are several ways to takes notes more effectively. I will give you a few methods. They are all using either pictures or words that will trigger what the speaker has been talking about. My hope is that you will be creative and come up with an additional method which is even more effective for you. Maybe it will be a combination of these. Put on your creative hat and do your best. Good luck!

The first is a circular process, by which all the information leads back to the middle of the circle. This can be done in words or pictures. The example on the next page is a diagram of "The Three Little Pigs." This is obviously done in pictures. Again, the same process can be done in words.

This next one done the same way, but in words. This is done on…You guess.

Now, there is another example of most of it, on the page following that works, too. Hey, any way that works for you is great; this is just another suggestion.

You set up your notes like this:

There are just a few words or pictures, but they will "*trigger*" what has happened in the story, so in the meantime, you can listen. If you review them quickly after your lecture, and then again at the end of the week, you will remember what they mean. This way you can do the "concentrating and focusing" exercise from Chapter Three while taking notes. Try this. If you are not in school now and you want to see if it works, then try it with a movie you watch on TV. It's amazing at how much you naturally forget, and how much you can remember with just a few triggers.

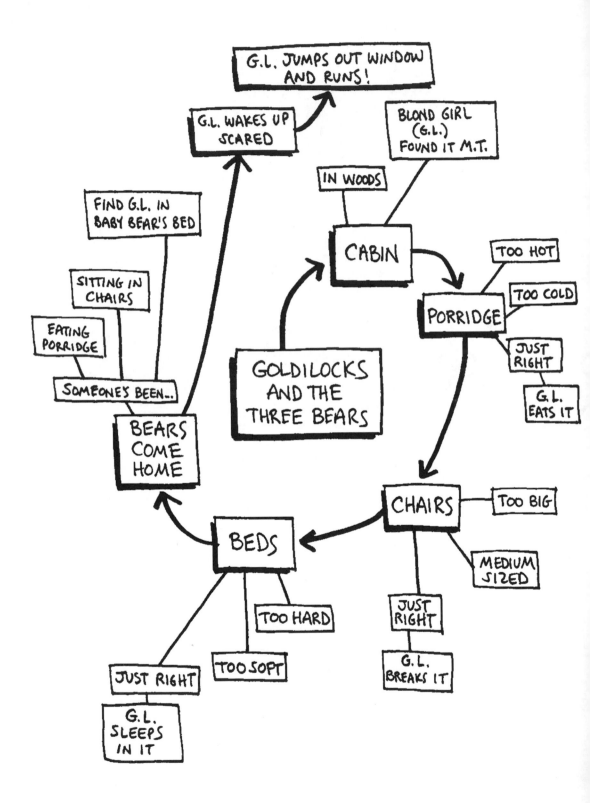

<u>Topic</u>	<u>Subtopics</u>	<u>Details</u>	<u>Miscellaneous</u>
Batman Episode	Bruce Wayne Batman's true identity Genius Weird personality Crusader for justice	Millionaire Meets blonde Fights street crime Drops Joker into acid Has affair Falls in love Gets revenge	Has big party

	Joker	Criminal
		Gets face melted by
		  acid
		Psychopathic
		Revenge against Bat-
		  man
		Chemical genius
		Falls in lust with
		  Newswoman
			Revenges boss
			Poison makeup
			Blonde woman
			Parade
			Church
			Death

	Newswoman	Gorgeous blonde
		Dedicated to story on
		  Batman
		Has an affair with
		  Batman
		Falls in love with
		  Batman
		Finds out the truth
		  about Bruce Wayne	

	Alfred	Lifetime companion
		  of Bruce Wayne
		Friend of Bruce and
		  his parents	

	Parents	Killed when he was a
		  boy, which made
		  him create Batman
		  to avenge his par-
		  ents. Parents killed
		  by the Joker when
		  Joker was a teen	

Why is it that triggers are so effective anyway? Do you know? Stop and think about this. It is *because you are creating a common association base*. Remember, when you associate something to your association base, it makes it easy to remember. Triggers are like this and they help make learning a breeze! So use key words or pictures that best remind you of what is being said.

The fewer words or pictures you need to use to remind you, the better.

What do these letters trigger for you? Give me a "B!" (Come on say these out loud with me.)

Now, give me a "B!"

Give me a "R!"

Give me an "E!"

Give me an "A!"

Give me a "K!"

What does it spell?...Well, take one!

Summary

Note taking can become easy when you use your imagination. You can draw or you can use words. You can take a complex lecture and make it easy by using the big picture technique. You start with the topic, then the subtopics, then the details. Then, you just fill anything else in that you may find important. You are the only one who can practice these methods, or another method you've created, to decide which one is most effective for you. You may combine a few of them and have pictures and words together. Remember, every method's right as long as it works for you!

Questions

1. What are the four categories for note taking?

_____

_____

_____

_____

2. Why would I only have three questions for this chapter?

_____

_____

_____

3. Write down two different methods of note taking.

_____

_____

TIMING   PACING   ENVIRONMENT

Chapter Eleven

How to Achieve the Greatest Results in the Least Amount of Time

Overview

By just practicing three simple methods, you will learn how, why, and when your brain works and operates most effectively. You will cut down considerably on study time, review time and frustration. These three words: "timing, pacing, and environment" are what made many students honor students without studying past 5:00 p.m. or on weekends. Would you like this to happen to you? It is possible. Read on.

Questions

1. You should study:
    A. Where you feel like it
    B. Where your environment enhances your learning
    C. Where your teachers tell you to study
    D. Both B and C

2. True or False? You start losing your retention level only ten minutes after you have heard something. _____

3. You really do have to study a lot if:
    A. You are stupid
    B. You want to retain information
    C. You study on your "off" time
    D. You want to succeed in life

4. True or False? If you are a morning person you must *always* study in the morning or don't study at all. _____

5. What is the shut-down mode?
   A. It's when it takes you at least twice as long to study something
   B. Your brain turns off completely
   C. When you are on information overload
   D. Both A and B

Many people think all they have to do is study a lot and they will do well. I used to think that, and it was a real drag. I'd rather play. What would you rather do? Would you like to study as little as possible and get awesome grades. Yes! That's how I feel. Are you with me? If you are, then, let's go! Read on....

Timing

The first thing I want to explain to you is how brains work pertaining to the time of day. So, I will begin by asking you a few questions:

When do you feel most alert?

Are you a morning person?

Are you an afternoon person?

Are you a night person?

"Are you a person? (Just kidding)"

You just experienced Hacker humor. As you can see, humor is one thing I didn't cover in the **EmpowerMind** course.

Now, on to the information I *do* cover. If you are a morning person, then the morning is your best time of day; it's when your mind is most alert. This is the time that you should study, work and do all of your important thinking. It is a time when you can accomplish ten times more than in your "off time."

Think about this a minute. If you are a morning person and you only study at night, it will take you so much longer to get the same amount accomplished, because your brain doesn't operate well at that time; it is on shut down mode. It's like trying to run a marathon with a sprained ankle; it's just not good timing. Think about a time when you studied on your "off time." Think about how you read a page and forgot what it said...immediately. Think about that. Also, think about how hard it is to remember when you are tired. Think about how many times you have to go over information again and again, when you are tired.

Let's simplify here. It is not a smart thing, to spend your time studying when you are in a "shut-down" mode. It takes you twice as long, with less effective results. When you study in your peak time, learning happens quickly. You can read and retain information at a much faster rate. You can think more effectively, so why would you persist in studying in shut-down mode times?

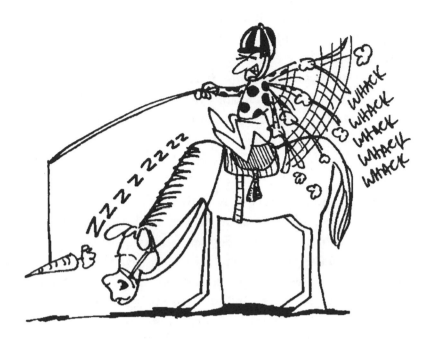

Shut-down mode can also happen when you are on what is called "information overload." This is when your mind has taken in about all it can, but you don't pay any attention to it. You just keep going. It is a time when you take twice as long to learn information. This is the time your body gets all tense because you can hardly stand to read another word.

"Kimberly, this is time for a pizza break or maybe a little "Saturday Night Live," where you can totally turn off your brain, dude."

Come back to it later; you'll accomplish twice as much when you are re-freshed. Your mind can go on forever, but your body is the culprit. It gets tired; it can only handle so much.

Ah-ha! Another real-life situation. If you are going to college, for instance, keep this strategy in mind when choosing your schedule. Ask yourself if it would be better for you to study during the day and take classes in the afternoon or night time. You can choose to take your study hour (if you have one) at your peak learning time of the day. It will truly catapult the amount of information you take in and retain.

This is what a friend of mine did in college. She went from a 2.3 to a 3.6 in one semester, by just using this method. She even skipped a few classes to study in her peak time. She had an exam coming up. She knew the teachers in the classes she skipped tested from the books and not the lectures. So, it made sense to spend her time where it was most effectively used. That time was best spent in studying (in her peak time) for her other test, in half the time it ordinarily would have taken her, if she had studied in her "off time." This is also an example of using the "big picture" method. You look over the whole situation and ask yourself: With all these variables and demands on me, how can I simplify the situation and make it all work? However, I don't advise you to do this in junior or senior high school. The negative effect of getting in trouble far outweighs studying at your peak time of day.

People spend so much wasted time in their lives forcing their brains to work harder than they need to work. When you get in touch with your physical cycle you will learn much quicker. Start asking yourself the question, "Which would be the most effective way to spend my time when studying? Is it when I am most alert, or do I need to compromise because of my schedule?" It is true that sometimes you won't have a choice. Sometimes, a test or quiz comes up at the last minute and you won't have enough time to prepare. Studying in your peak time is for when you have an option to choose. Sometimes, you can create your options too, but sometimes you are limited and need to make the best of what conditions you have available.

Pacing

Next, I want you to understand how pacing can also aid you in your learning process. Most importantly, how it can continue to take off more of your study time.

First, you need to know a few things. The chart on the next page will show you how your brain retains information. As you can see, from this study that Tony Buzan writes about in his book, *Use Both Sides of Your Brain*, you lose informa-tion quickly. It's important now to know what to do with this information.

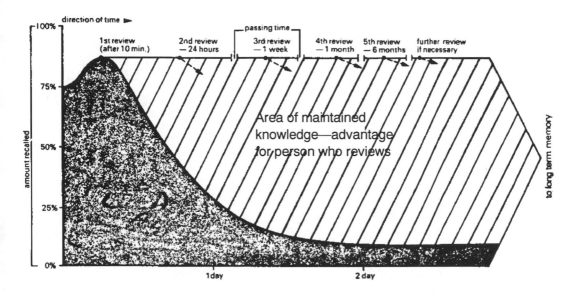

Time Elapsed After Receiving Information
From "Use Both Sides of Your Brain," by Tony Buzan

You remember more ten minutes after you have learned something. Why do you think you learn more then? Your subconscious is making associations to the information you just acquired. Then, as you can see, it slides fast. Hacker knows this concept.

"Isn't that depressing?"

Well, it really isn't, *if* you know how your brain works and how to use it to your advantage.

1. All you have to do, when you leave a lecture, is to mentally review it on your way out of the lecture.
2. Then, do a quick review of your notes, taken the **EmpowerMind** way, of course.
3. Then, review them quickly before bed. Your subconscious can work on the information while you sleep.
4. Then, review once more at the end of each week (or a specific day that *you* choose each week).
5. Then, review it once more before your final exams.

Tony Buzan also shows how quickly we lose information.

Direction of time   →

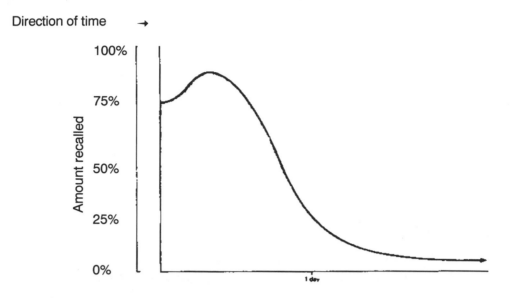

When you review quickly, over and over again, you bring up your retention level. It's also easier to access information when you learned it a day ago, versus three weeks ago. This way, by the time final exams come, you only have to do another quick review and not spend a lot of time re-learning everything. Doesn't this make sense? Try it and you will know the answer. You agreed that you didn't want to spend a lot of time studying to get good grades. Well then, this is the way. Every time you review, it will take hours off your study time. You will keep all the information fresh, so you don't have to re-learn it again.

Another very important part of pacing is to study in short intervals. If your brain can only pay attention for approximately nine minutes at a time, it makes sense for you to study the same thing in the same way for about that same amount of time.

For example, you may be learning a foreign language and you have vocabulary and grammar to learn. You might learn the definitions to ten of the vocabulary words, stand up take a quick two-minute break then come back and work ten minutes on the grammar. You may do this over and over until you get it. Or simply study one subject for ten minutes, then a different one, and then go back to the original subject.

You might also learn facts and figures while taking a walk in nature. You simply carry some notes in your pocket, look at them, then think about them and your associations while walking. Repeat them over and over again. It's relaxing, it gives you variety and stimulation, and it's good exercise to relieve tension.

"This is my opinion, as the Hacker dude. Your brain will say, come on guys, let's go! This is a piece of cake now!"

In fact, I tutored Brandon in his tree fort. He was climbing away while learning a speech. He was so active that it was hard for him to sit still to learn subjects and to memorize. When he was moving he was so stimulated that it became easy for him to focus on the subject matter and repeat the speech to me. Then he climbed down and delivered the speech to me in two different places in his yard. His speech was awesome! His attention was on it, he presented it well with great retention and the bonus was that it was fun!

Attention teachers! *I know* you cannot allow climbing and constant running around in your classrooms. But, you can have your students switching seats, working in pairs, act out the subject matter; and you can also lecture from different sides of the room, etc. You can create whatever you choose. You are in control. Try it! Your students will love it and the results will speak for themselves.

I have found that when the rhythm is changed and the pacing of the subject matter is changed, the students can better receive and retain the information. They need to hear it and think about it, then they need to have an experience with it, then they need to repeat it to a partner, explaining what they just learned. If a student can explain what he or she just learned or teach it to another student, then the magic truly occurs; the student learns and remembers.

"Attention students! You can take responsibility too. You can take notes at one point, listen with pictures in your mind at a another point, mimic the teacher at another point (in your mind of course), have a personal experience with the subject matter in your

Quick Reviews

life or in your imagination, sit in a different seat each day (if it's allowed). You can repeat what you just learned to a friend or set up a buddy system to teach each other. Man, if ya' can teach it or repeat it back, you've got it!"

You always want to change the material or the way you are learning it, or you'll want to change the environment you're learning it in. It automatically stimulates your brain to absorb and retain information.

Environment

The last of these three magical ingredients is "Environment." This is very simple. Do you study best at home? In a library, in a classroom, on a ski boat, on the beach...? Only you can decide where you study best and what environment you need to study in. Choosing the place you study is the first step.

Now you need to have the proper lighting. If you have bad lighting, then your eyes will get tired, because they have to work harder. Remember, this is all about working easier.

Don't let anyone tell you that you cannot study with music on. Sometimes it helps. Some people study well with the sound of waves or instrumental music in the background.

"I, Hacker, wouldn't advise acid rock and loud rap music as the answer. I know, I tried them both, when I learned music could be a positive influence in studying. I guess it's supposed to be relaxing music."

I would not recommend studying at the beach either, but there are audio tapes out there that can make you feel as though you are on the beach. Remember, *imagination, imagination, imagination!*

Make sure you are in a comfortable chair and that you are not distracted by your surroundings. Right, Hacker?

"Like studying in the middle of a party might not be a good idea. Is that what you're saying Kimberly?"

Yes, and in addition, make sure your body is taken care of properly. Your stomach should be full (ever try to study on an empty stomach?)

"Make sure you eat lots of sugar and soda pop so you can be completely wired and in your beta state...Not!"

Hacker! What you eat makes a big difference. Everybody is a little different, but generally, red meat makes people tired. It takes a long time to digest. If you eat candy or sugar, you will get a boost of energy, then crash! Think about which classes you lose your energy in. Have you had a sugar snack right before them? The best things to eat before and while studying would be (yep, you guessed it) vegetables and fruits. Keep them at your study place, so you don't have to get up and distract yourself.

If you get tired and you know you have a ways to go yet, then stand up, wave your hands above your head and snort like a pig. Hey, you'll loosen up, and it will make you laugh. It should revitalize you. I'd just like to be there when your friends walk in the room and see you. Go walk around if you need to. Rub your shoulders and tell yourself how great you are doing. Rub both of your ears at the same time; this will stimulate both sides of your brain. And, always program yourself to finish in minutes versus hours and hours versus days.

If your environment gets dull you can change it every ten minutes or whenever you feel you are losing your attention. You might have two or three places set up for studying and rotate through all of them. Remember you are in control of the experience. You can create whatever you choose to make your environment(s) the best possible place(s) to learn.

Well, what do you think? Do you think this makes sense? Hey, I may not have a Ph.D. in school, but I certainly have it in results. You will too, if you "just do it!"

Summary

All three of these techniques—Timing, Pacing and Environment—are important. If you learn when your mind is most alert, how often you need to review information and which environment is most conducive for receiving information, you will rapidly speed your learning and retention levels. This means less study time and more play time!

Questions

1. You should study:
   A. Where you feel like it
   B. Where your environment enhances your learning
   C. Where your teachers tell you to study
   D. Both B and C

2. True or False? You start losing your retention level only ten minutes after you have heard something. _____

3. You really do have to study a lot if:
   A. You are stupid
   B. You want to retain information
   C. You study on your "off" time
   D. You want to succeed in life

4. True or False? If you are a morning person you must *always* study in the morning or don't study at all. _____

5. What is the shut-down mode?
   A. It's when it takes you at least twice as long to study something
   B. Your brain turns off completely
   C. When you are on information overload
   D. Both A and B
   E. Both A and C

6. Sometimes it's good to:
   A. Over study
   B. Skip class, in an extreme situation
   C. Study on the beach in the middle of summer
   D. Drink lots of caffeine and eat sugar for a boost

7. You should review mentally:
   A. Right after class
   B. Right before the exam
   C. When you feel like it
   D. When you are trying to impress someone

8. You should practice the Timing, Pacing, and Environment techniques because: _____

   _____

   _____

9. The suggestions on environment deal with:
   A. Recycling
   B. Being conscious of your environment while studying, this means don't throw out anything
   C. Keeping your environment for studying very clean
   D. Creating an environment that is effective for you, while studying

10. When you get tired, while studying you can:
    A. Stand up, put your arms over your head and snort like a pig
    B. Rub your ears
    C. Stand up and walk around
    D. Just take a break
    E. All of the above

Congratulations! That's it! You are done. You are an **EmpowerMind** graduate. Did it go by fast? I hope you had as much fun reading and participating in the missions, exercises and games as I had writing them. I hope Hacker was a helpful peer to you students. But most of all, I hope you all have more tools to help you become happier in your life and achieve what *you* want to achieve to become successful (whatever successful means to *you*). If you are interested in additional materials or services, the following are available: Tapes, workshops, speeches and tutoring. If there is anything else I can do or any way in which I can be of service to you, your friends and school or workplace, please FAX me at 415-389-6941 or write to **EmpowerMind**, 38 Miller Ave., Suite 201, Mill Valley, CA 94941. I'll look forward to hearing from you.

Now, go...go out and be a positive example to others. Explore new worlds... Live the **EmpowerMind** way... Just do it!

Answers to Chapter Questions

Chapter One

1. Learning
2. Nothing
3. True
4. Experiences
5. E
6. Learn names, teach something, more empathy for other students, communicate differently, etc.
7. Think in cartoons or pictures. Pretend the situation is different than it really is.
8. B
9. Engrain it, Mention it, Play with it, Overplay it, Wait for an association, Exaggerate it, Review or Repeat it
10. A
11. Language

Chapter Two

1. Pictures
2. E
3. A
4. F
5. C
6. D
7. Yes, by imagining a picture of what the word reminds you of and doing the same with the meaning of the word. Then, you attach the two pictures together.
8. Yes, if it looks like a number, it's right!
9. Any attachment of pictures between the vocabulary word and its meaning will work.
10. D
11. A

Chapter Three

1. B
2. C
3. Repeating or imitating or copying what someone is saying or doing
4. D
5. T
6. D
7. Because it naturally reminds us of what we're trying to recall.
8. Cheat Sheets
9. F
10. Yes
11. A
12. Something different than both or either of you are; actual examples are O.K.

Chapter Four

1. F
2. Imagination, Reality or what is not real and what is real
3. D
4. E
5. D
6. D
7. D
8. T
9. A
10. A
11. Subconscious
12. A
13. A
14. T
15. Good to it.

Chapter Five

1. Missiles, microwaves, TV, satellites etc.
2. D
3. D
4. C
5. When you need an answer to a question
6. When you want to achieve a goal (examples are O.K., too)
7. T
8. B
9. Alpha/Beta
10. D, because it's alpha/beta

Chapter Six

1. D
2. T
3. E
4. Fear
5. Any seven of the twelve steps are correct. (It doesn't need to be word for word.)

Chapter Seven

1. A
2. D
3. B
4. Moment
5. Laugh (or smile), Fun
6. D
7. T
8. F
9. C
10. When we notice everything around us, we're generally calmer. We're experiencing things for what they are, not for what they seem to be. We're happier.
11. Money
12. B
13. C
14. A
15. T

Chapter Eight

1. F
2. Fear (half credit for hate), Love
3. T
4. Zero
5. D
6. Limitless
7. F
8. T
9. C
10. Try to feel love for everything. Keep talking yourself into it. Say, "I LOVE" each thing you experience that day. Say it out loud to convince yourself.
11. Receive
12. Compassion
13. F
14. Love
15. Human

Chapter Nine

1. Imagination, Reality
2. C,D,B,A
3. 3-5 weeks
4. T
5. A
6. Imagination
7. T
8. It is a sign we're going in the right direction
9. C
10. Yes, by empowering people to see their potential, by giving them compassion and support.
11. B
12. A
13. Any examples of an athlete seeing success and going into the alpha state before the event can work.
14. T
15. What, When, Why, Where, How, With Whom
16. F

17. Yourself, and those who have supported you along the way
18. Time limit
19. People you respect for advice
20. "I can do it!" Or "I won't give up!" It doesn't have to be verbatim.

Chapter Ten

1. Big Picture, Subtopics, Details, Miscellaneous information
2. Because it's short
3. Pictures, Columns, Boxes

Chapter Eleven

1. B
2. T
3. C
4. F
5. E
6. B (Re-read what I meant by this)
7. A
8. You can study less and retain more
9. D
10. E

RESOURCES

   This section has been formed to give you greater support. It includes categories of books and resources which will provide you with a greater depth of knowledge in each area of learning and life. This book and my life have been enhanced greatly, by many of these resources.

Goal Setting and Motivational

Unlimited Power, Anthony Robbins, Ballantine Books, 1986. Also available in audio tapes.

Wish Craft, Barbara Sher with Annie Gottlieb, Ballantine Books, 1983. This is especially great for gaining more resources. I have included a few from their book.

What Color Is Your Parachute? Richard N. Bolles. Ten Speed Press, P.O. Box 7123, Berkeley, CA 94707

Follow Your Bliss, Hal Zina Bennett, Ph.D. and Susan J. Sparrow, Avon Books, 1990

Live Your Dreams, Les Brown, Morrow & Co., Inc., 1992. Also available in audio tapes.

Do It!, John-Roger and Peter Mcwilliams, Prelude Press, 1991.

Creative Thinking and Problem Solving:

A Whack On The Side Of The Head, Roger Von Oech, self-published, 1983.

Unicorns Are Real: A Right-Brained Approach To Learning, Barbara Meister Vitale, Jalmar Press 1982.

The Book Of Think, Marilyn Burns, The Yolla Bolly Press 1976.

Study Skills and Memory Techniques

How To Get Better Grades And Have More Fun, Steve Douglas with Al Johnson, Here's Life Publishers Inc. 1985.

Memory Dynamics Institute P.O. Box 13592, 4125 Industrial Road., Las Vegas Nevada 89112, 800-RECALL-8 Available in audio tapes.

How the Brain Operates

Use Both Sides Of Your Brain, Tony Buzan, Penguin Group, 1991.

Brain Power, Karl Albrecht, Simon & Schuster, 1992.

You're Smarter Than You Think, Seymour Epstein Ph.D. with Archie Brodsky, Simon & Schuster 1993.

Human Relations and Effective Communication

How To Win Friends And Influence People, Dale Carnegie, Simon & Schuster Revised edition, 1981.

How Can I Help, Ram Dass and Paul Gorman, Alfred A. Knopf, Inc. 1985

Men Are From Mars, Women Are From Venus, John Gray, Harper Collins, 1992.

My Feelings, My Self, Lynda Madaras with Area Madaras, New Market Press, 1993. It's written for teenagers.

Effective Teaching and Instruction

Comments On Exceptional Instruction, L. Gray Burdin, Dale Carnegie & Associates, Inc. 1975

Self-Improvement and Self-Help

The Quick and Easy Way To Effective Speaking, Dorthy Carnegie, Dale Carnegie and Associates, Inc.

Don't Grow Old—Grow Up, Dorthy Carnegie, Dale Carnegie and Associates, Inc.

What to Say When You Talk To Yourself and *The Self-Talk Solution*, Shad Helmstetter, William Morrow & Co, 1987.

Forgiveness, Dr. Sidney B. Simon and Suzanne Simon, Philip Lief Group Inc., 1990.

Teenage Esteem, Dr. Pat Palmer with Melissa Froehner, Impact, 1989.

Teens Talk About Alcohol And Alcoholism edited, Paul Dolmetsch and Gail Mauricette.

Spirituality

The Road Less Traveled, M. Scott Peck, Simon & Schuster 1978

Handbook to Higher Consciousness, Ken Keyes, Jr., The Living Love Center, 1975

A Course In Miracles, Foundation for Inner Peace, Foundation for Inner Peace, 1992.

Return To Love, Marianne Williamson, Harper Collins, 1992. Also available in audio tapes.

The Peaceful Warrior, Dan Millman, H.J. Kramer, Inc.,1984. Also Available in audio tapes.

Ageless Body Timeless Mind, Deepak Chopra M.D. Harmony Books, 1993.

The Celestine Prophecy, James Redfield, Warner Brothers Inc. 1993.

The Vision, Tom Brown, Jr. The Berkley Publishing Group, 1988.

Mutant Message Downunder, Marlo Morgan, MM Co., 1991.

Overcoming Fear

How to Stop Worrying And Start Living, Dale Carnegie, Simon & Schuster Revised edition.

Stop Running Scared, Herbert Fensterheim and Jean Baer.

Feel The Fear And Do It Anyway, Susan Jeffers, Ballantine Books, 1987

Love is Letting Go Of Fear, Gerald Jampolsky, M.D.

Teenage Stress, Eileen Kalberg Van Wie, Julian Messner, 1987.

A Life Without Fear, Laura C. Martin, Rutledge Hill Press, 1992.

Educational Games

WFF'N PROOF Learning Games (Instructional Gaming Program), 1490 South Blvd. Ann Arbor Michigan 48104 (313) 665 2269

The Human Calculator featuring Scott Flansburg, 1991 Media Arts International 1875 Campus Commons Dr. Suite 200 Reston, Virginia 22091 (Tapes and Workbook)

Internships and Apprenticeships

Career Internship Program, Carol Feit Lane, 115 E. 87 St. in New York, NY 10028 212-831-7930

Fast Forward Newspaper (for teenagers), John McCloud 79 Walnut St. Mill Valley, CA 94941 (415) 381-8230

National Apprenticeship Program, US Department of Labor, Manpower Administration, Washington D.C. 20210

Nontraditional Employment for Women, 105 E. 22nd St., New York NY 10010

(212) 420-0060 Helps women get apprenticeships in unionized non-traditional women trades, e.g., carpentry, machinist trade, etc.

Vocational Instruction

How to Sell Your Artwork, Milton K. Berlye. Prentice-Hall

Opportunities in Acting, Vocational Guidance manuals, 620 Fifth St., Louisville KY 40202

Courses and/or Workshops and Retreats

EmpowerMind Workshop, Kimberly Kassner & Associates, 38 Miller Ave., Suite 201, Mill Valley, CA 94941 (FAX: 415-389-6941). A personal experience with the book contents and much more.

Seeing the Light, Brain integration training, 825 Gravenstein Hwy. North, Suite 3, Sebastopol, CA 95472, (707) 824-9037. Training on how to become integrated emotionally, spiritually, and physically. You will learn to become fusionally integrated.

The Learning Forum Foundation (Super Camp), 1725 S. Hill St., Oceanside, CA 92054-5319. A camp that teaches study skills and more.

The Pacific Process, The Institute for Personal Progress and Change 2295 Palou, San Francisco 94124 415-550-6410. A thirteen week process to help eliminate negative programming from your childhood.

The Dale Carnegie Course, Dale Carnegie & Associates, Inc. 1475 Franklin Ave. Garden City, NY 11530. A human relations and public speaking course. (Courses offered across the United States.)

Meditation One-Four, Center for Intuitive Development 20 Sunnyside #236-A Mill Valley, CA 94941, (415) 388-6524. A six week to two year process in helping you becoming more intuitive, relaxed and self-aware.

Hamsa Institute, A-118 Mill Valley, CA 94941 (415) 389-0214. Individual coaching on how to become clear about your issues and steps given to eliminate them. Also trust building, ropes courses and self-awareness retreats outdoors.

Voyager—Outward Bound School, Mill Place 120, 111 3rd Ave., S. Minneapolis, MN 55401, (612) 338-0131. This is a school that offers a course/retreat in the wilderness, which helps youth gain courage, self-esteem, confidence and independence. This is achieved, by taking them into the wilderness and helping them get in touch with the natural elements, which provide both spiritual enlightenment and great physical and mental challenges.

An Income of Her Own, P.O. Box 8452, San Jose, CA 95155-8452, (408) 295-7083. The aim of this program is to impact the long term financial well being, self-esteem, and expectations of young women, by introducing girls to the possibilities of entrepreneurship as a leadership vehicle and a career option.

Order form for additional books and tapes

Please send _____ book(s) and _____ relaxation/visualization tape(s) to:

Name: _____

Address: _____

_____

Enclosed is $19.95 per book and $11.95 per tape for a total of $ _____
     Note: Deduct 20% on orders of 5 or more books and tapes
     (can include any combination of books and tapes)

Shipping and handling: $2.00 for the first book; $.75 for each addl. $ _____

No shipping or handling charge for a single tape; $.50 for each addl. $ _____

California residents only; add 7.75% sales tax $ _____

                                 Total enclosed $ _____

Method of payment:

    ☐ Check   ☐ Money Order   ☐ Visa /Master Card

Account #_____

Ex. Date _____ Signature _____

Mail to:

EmpowerMind
38 Miller Avenue, Suite 201
Mill Valley, CA 94941

☐ Please include information on **EmpowerMind** courses in my area.

Thank you and keep on learning!

Order form for additional books and tapes

Please send _____ book(s) and _____ relaxation/visualization tape(s) to:

Name: _____

Address: _____

_____

Enclosed is $19.95 per book and $11.95 per tape for a total of $ _____
    Note: Deduct 20% on orders of 5 or more books and tapes
    (can include any combination of books and tapes)

Shipping and handling: $2.00 for the first book; $.75 for each addl. $ _____

No shipping or handling charge for a single tape; $.50 for each addl. $ _____

California residents only; add 7.75% sales tax $ _____

                             Total enclosed $ _____

Method of payment:

☐ Check   ☐ Money Order   ☐ Visa /Master Card

Account # _____

Ex. Date _____ Signature _____

Mail to:

EmpowerMind
38 Miller Avenue, Suite 201
Mill Valley, CA 94941

☐ Please include information on **EmpowerMind** courses in my area.

Thank you and keep on learning!